Praise for
The Findability Formula

"In the brave new world of SEO and SEM, Heather Lutze and Lutze Consulting bring valuable Internet insights and experience to the marketing arena. Forward-thinking advertising and marketing professionals should take advantage of this tried-and-true marketing knowledge of the digital universe."
—Pasquale Marranzino, Chairman and CEO,
Karsh & Hagan Advertising

"The Findability Formula simplifies the complex world of Internet marketing. Every business will benefit from understanding simple to advanced techniques for finding new customers online."
—Brad Geddes, Google AdWords trainer and BG theory consultant

"After many failed attempts at search engine marketing, we are now back on track and on the top of search results—thanks to The Findability Formula, *a must-read!"*
—Michael A. DeMayo, Law Offices of Michael A. DeMayo, LLP,
Charlotte, North Carolina

"The Findability Formula is a must-read for all people or organizations that are trying to establish themselves on the Internet. Heather Lutze provides an easy-to-use process that works. Her information is useful, practical, and it produces results. If you want to be found on the Web, this is the book you need to read."
—Ron Karr, CSP, President, Karr & Associates, Inc.

"In this book Heather has taken complicated paid marketing concepts and translated them into real business strategies that every business owner should pay attention to if they want to grow their online presence."
—Sean A. Golliher, Founder/Publisher
Search Engine Marketing Journal

The Findability Formula

The Findability Formula

The Easy, Non-Technical Approach to Search Engine Marketing

Heather Lutze

WILEY

John Wiley & Sons, Inc.

For general information on our other products and services or for technical support,
please contact our Customer Care Department within the United States at (800) 762-2974,
outside the United States at (317) 572-3993 or fax (317) 572-4002.

Wiley also publishes its books in a variety of electronic formats. Some content that appears
in print may not be available in electronic books. For more information about Wiley
products, visit our web site at www.wiley.com.

Library of Congress Cataloging-in-Publication Data:
Lutze, Heather, 1969–
    The findability formula : the easy, non-technical approach to search
  engine marketing / Heather Lutze.
        p.   cm.
    Includes bibliographical references and index.
    ISBN 978-0-470-42090-4 (pbk.)
    1. Internet marketing.   2. Internet advertising.   3. Internet searching.
  4. Web search engines.   I. Title.
  HF5415.1265.L88 2009
  658.8'72–dc22
                                                                2008038668
Printed in the United States of America.

10 9 8 7 6 5 4 3 2 1

Contents

Foreword

There are few things more frustrating than doing an Internet search for your *own name* and not even turning up in the results, especially if your livelihood depends on it. After writing a half-dozen books and touring the lecture circuit for 30 years, I'm at least almost famous, yet there was my web site, buried on the twelfth page.

These days, if your site doesn't turn up "above the fold," that is, within the first five or six results of a search, you might as well not even exist. They think you died, if they think of you at all. In my business, I AM the product, so I hired a geek, spent thousands of dollars and several months of late nights rebuilding my web site. We managed to move it from 124th to 56th. Depressing.

When it comes to being found, the Internet has evolved into the world's ultimate haystack. It's made up of more than 180 *million* web sites and *billions* of pages of text, images, and video. And it's growing at the rate of 1.3 million *new* web sites a month (http://news.netcraft.com/archives/web_server_survey.html).

Luckily for us, smart people have developed clever software that sifts through this whole mess, so we can find the information we want with just a few keystrokes (well, usually), and "Google" has become a verb.

Good content and good design used to be enough to get you found. But all the search engines have different methods of deciding what constitutes a match, and the rules keep changing. Like a lot of people today, I was lost in the labyrinth of HTML meta tags, keywords, and reciprocal links; and if it's not all done just right, you're actually penalized. So my gorgeous, expensive, Flash-powered, content-rich, e-commerce-enabled web site wasn't even getting on the radar.

Making it all even more complicated, the search entrepreneurs realized they could charge good money to make your site leapfrog to the top of the page, and companies lined up to pay millions to ensure their findability. Speaker bureaus were waging a bidding war, running pay per click ads to divert searchers who had looked for me BY NAME over to their own web sites, where they could sell the services of some other schmuck who wasn't nearly as good.

That's when I was introduced to Heather Lutze. Heather is a fellow member of the National Speakers Association, and she lectures on this topic all over the country, so we hit it off right away. She has been managing the Internet ad campaigns of hundreds of companies, large and small, for years. She is SO intense and knowledgeable. Heather became my guide.

Luckily for me, Heather has cracked the code on search engine optimization. She gave my site a thorough shakedown, making dozens of quick-fix recommendations that we could implement right away. We set up an AdWords campaign, so we could see exactly how people search when they're looking for a speaker on "Guerrilla Selling." We set up alerts to automatically notify us when new, competing content was published, and we tested various headlines and taglines to track where the clicks were coming from. The results were an eye-opener; they were nothing like what we had assumed.

When she asked me to read the first few chapters of this book before submission, it was like the clouds parted and the sun came out. I GOT it! Heather has a gift for cutting through all the jargon, so it wasn't complicated and it wasn't difficult. Once you understand how your customers LOOK for you online, building a web site that gets FOUND is straightforward and easy. You begin to attract the RIGHT customers, RIGHT when they're ready to buy.

Together, we used all the data to inform a complete redesign of my site, with smarter architecture and a more straightforward selling cycle. We loaded it with content rich in keywords using our customers' vocabulary instead of our own. And we upped the ante on our pay per click, bringing in qualified inquiries from hot prospects. And the results were unbelievable. I'm getting found. I'm getting booked. I'm getting PAID.

Finding your own "findability formula" is like having a license to print money. And you'll see it explained here in simple, non-technical terms that non-geeks like me can understand.

ORVEL RAY WILSON, CSP
Author of best-selling book *Guerrilla Selling*
www.GuerrillaGroup.com

Acknowledgments

A heartfelt thank-you goes out to my entire *Findability Formula* book team because without you, this book would never have been possible. Thanks to my amazing husband Mark and my sons, Evan and Kyle, for putting up with my long nights and endless edits; to my amazing copywriter Maury for her unending energy and enthusiasm; to Cindy for her "get-to-the-finish-line" technical help; and last but not least, to my mom because without her "you should write a book" dream for me, it would never have come true. I am blessed to have you all in my life.

Introduction

Who Should Read This Book?

The Findability Formula is written for businesses that market themselves on the Internet but aren't quite satisfied with their results. It's also the perfect book for those of you who are about to embark on a search engine marketing program but want to avoid making mistakes and wasting money. This book will not only save you time and money; it will also exponentially improve your results.

Additionally, *The Findability Formula* will also help those of you who already know that being found by common search engines—the very definition of "findability"—is critical to Internet marketing success; but who need to learn how to improve your search engine rankings.

If you're a total novice, this book is perfect for you. We recommend that you read the entire book before starting the paid-search process. It will help you avoid the disastrous mistakes so many advertisers make.

If you're a paid search advertiser who is frustrated with your results, this book will make a significant difference in your success. I meet hundreds of paid search advertisers over the course of a year, and I'm often surprised at the basic mistakes made by experienced advertisers—even at large and sophisticated companies. This book will help you correct or avoid some of those errors, and get your campaigns performing as you hoped they would.

If you're mystified by search engine optimization (SEO) and can't figure out how to get your site "organically" ranked, *The Findability Formula* will unlock the secrets to identifying the keywords and search terms under which you want to be found. It will also help you understand the intricate relationship between paid search and SEO.

If you're a seasoned search marketer who is well experienced with search marketing, you may find the language and approach of the book a little elementary for your level of experience. However, I guarantee that you'll find new ideas, tips, and fresh approaches for taking your paid search campaigns to the next level.

When I'm training, I almost always encounter a few crossed arm, closed-face, resistant people who are certain that they already know everything that there is to know about search marketing, and that there's nothing new anyone can teach them. You can tell that they're not happy about having to sit through my training. Yet 9 times out of 10, these are the very people who come up to me at the end of the day to say thank-you, and to tell me that they had learned some useful new things.

I've been involved in search marketing since 1998, and *I* still learn something new every day. I'm constantly refining my skills and the campaigns that I manage—including my own. So I suggest that experienced advertisers read this book with what Zen Buddhists refer to as the "beginner's mind"—a mindset that is open to new ideas.

The Findability Formula includes creative strategies for keeping campaigns fresh and performing. It offers approaches to help you find new ideas and get out of your comfort zone, so that you can reenergize stale campaigns. It's easy for successful search marketing managers to get too comfortable with the same old keywords or their favorite ads; after all, sometimes you just run out of ideas. This book will provide input for tweaking campaigns so they're even more successful.

If you're a "techie" you could learn a lot from reading this book. Even though *The Findability Formula* isn't a technical guide, you might enjoy the novel approach of looking at search marketing from the *customer's* perspective.

Finally, *if you're hiring an agency* to manage your search engine marketing, this book will be a useful resource. You're going to want to monitor what they're doing and closely track the results they're getting because no one knows your business and your customers as well as you do. What you learn here will also help protect you from common mistakes that agencies often make and that end up costing you money. Without recounting a lot of horror stories, suffice it to say that it's not a good idea to be too hands-off with your search marketing agency.

For all readers, the purpose of this book is to help you crack the code of *being visible to your customers* when they are *searching* on the Internet and when they *ready to buy.* It will teach you how to *appropriately connect* with customers throughout their search process, especially when they are ready to take *action.* This is the formula anyone marketing a business on the Internet wants to know and understand.

If you read the entire book—and we've kept it short to make that easy to do—you'll discover that it gives you the fundamentals and the practical steps for the deployment of a paid search campaign. It shows you how to translate what you learn into a productive, organic, SEO-friendly strategy that gets results.

You'll see exactly how paid search works, and also how to make it work *with* organic search to create optimum web visibility and reduce paid search costs over time.

We'll walk you step-by-step through search engine marketing from the ground up, including:

- Creating a paid search (*pay per click* or *PPC*) campaign from scratch, or redoing your existing campaigns
- Demystifying SEO by teaching you how to connect with searchers under the correct keyword phrases when they are ready to buy—*no guesswork involved*
- Explaining how the two approaches to search marketing (paid search and SEO) relate to each other, and how they work together to optimize your presence on the web

We will illuminate the art and science of making a business visible on the Internet—*the formula for findability*—and for *converting prospects to purchasers.* If that's what you want, then this book is for you.

How This Book Is Different

The Findability Formula is different from other search marketing books in three important ways:

1. It's written in *plain English.* We're not diving into coding or other technical stuff, and we're not talking theory. We're offering *practical steps* to get your site *found on the Internet;* and we're using understandable and down-to-earth language that *any businessperson can easily follow* to walk you through the process.

2. We teach you the art of *finding the keywords* that will spell online success for your business because **keywords are the key to the findability formula.** (By the way, your highest performing keywords are often not the ones you might guess.)

3. Although this book is about how to be found on the Internet through the search engines, it is also about how to respond to your **customers** and understand *their* issues, *their* wants, and *their* needs. It explains how you can connect with them along every step of their "path to purchase."

One of the basic flaws in search marketing—a mistake made by amateurs and professionals alike—is that they put too much emphasis on the search engines and not enough on the customer experience. This is a serious error.

I'd been observing this problem for quite some time, when I had an "a-ha!" moment during a meeting with a well-known search engine and a fundamental search marketing error suddenly became clear.

The "Secret Agent" Pen Story

For our quarterly meeting with one of our major search engine partners (who shall remain nameless), some big corporate guns flew in from out of town. They ordered a fancy breakfast and made a PowerPoint presentation that detailed my company's spending with them over the past nine years, how much traffic we had generated, and our overall success with their search marketing tools. At the end of the meeting, they announced that they had a gift for me to express their appreciation for all the business I had sent their way. They mentioned that it came from their "VIP gift collection."

With a bit of flourish, they handed me a small, nicely wrapped box that I imagined might contain a diamond watch or perhaps airline tickets to an exotic location. I got kind of excited wondering how a company of their size might reward a client who had spent more then a few million dollars with them.

Inside the package there was a very fancy James Bond-style brushed aluminum case, which I opened with great anticipation; and there, nestled in its custom-fit foam bed, I found . . . a *pen.*

Now, don't get me wrong; it was a very cool pen. A sort of space-age, *Get Smart* kind of pen with a laser pointer, a flashlight, and USB port. But folks, it was a pen! Nine years and millions dollars, and I got a pen.

At that moment, it struck me: *we've got this thing all wrong.*

Search marketers spend all their time courting the search engines, but they're focusing on the wrong people. Luckily, the "pen incident" woke me from the search engine stupor. It was the clearest illustration possible that if you spend all your time focused on the search engines, you've misspent your time, energy, and search marketing efforts.

What we need to do is to focus on our customers.

I'd been killing myself to build relationships with the search engines, and what was my reward in the end? A pen. Don't get me wrong; I'm not ungrateful. It was very nice of the search engine to acknowledge me, given that they have millions of customers. And I absolutely appreciate my relationship with them and how wonderfully they support me and my clients. But fundamentally, since I am paying them to perform a service they are really working for me, not the other way around. In that moment, it woke me up to this realization:

We need to court our customers—not the search engines . . . our customers!

And what's our reward for that? Business! And sales! And profits.

It's time for us all to shift our concentration from the search engines to our customers—the people who actually give us business. Search engines are amazing conduits that connect us with customers all over the world, but online success lies in our ability to meet the needs and requirements of our *customers*, not the search engines. This shift in focus will drastically change your online business.

And in a neat twist of fate, if you create a great user experience, then the search engines reward you with good positioning and ranking anyway.

So we're going to teach you how to uncover the keywords that will **connect** you with your prospects throughout every stage of their Internet search process. We're also going to share the secret to servicing them in such a way that they **convert to paying customers.**

Our SEM consulting practice clients pay big bucks for this information—and you're getting it for just the price of this book.

If you execute what you learn here, you will avoid making the mistakes that multitudes of business owners make every day, and my reward will be knowing that I have made an important contribution to your search marketing success. (And that beats even the fanciest pen, any day!)

Take-Away

- At the conclusion of each chapter, we will include the most important "Take-Aways" from that chapter. We hope you will find this helpful.

About the Author

Heather Lutze was working with the Internet before many of us even knew what the Internet was. She's as savvy as they come.
—Tom Harper, "The Food Guy"

Before reading this book, you probably want to know who I am, and exactly what makes me an authority on Internet marketing.

I began my career as a web designer. After I sold my web development company, I became the Internet Marketing Manager at a large dot-com in Denver, Colorado, and was responsible for implementing a multimillion-dollar Internet marketing budget. This was prior to the infamous dot-com bust of the late 1990s.

My job was to "brand" the company on the Internet prior to our IPO (Initial Public Offering). It was a race to the finish line to spend

$2.5 million as quickly as possible to impress potential investors and support the IPO.

This was before pay per click advertising existed; Internet advertising was uncharted territory and a bit of a free-for-all. Metrics were all about "traffic," "hits," "eyeballs," and "CPM" (cost per thousand). Banner ads, display ads, contextual ads, and pop-ups were all popular vehicles. We didn't match venues to target audience; we simply bought display ads on any and all web sites. I remember we once spent $50,000 to be on the front page of Yahoo.com, on which our ad appeared for exactly one day. Those were the kinds of buys we were making: *$50,000 for one day!* At the time, that was perfectly acceptable. We were just after traffic and hits, and we had no method to any of the madness. We were just trying everything. Our instructions were simple: *"Get eyeballs on the site. Build brand awareness at any cost. Now go!"*

It turns out, however, that no one should have cared about traffic and hits. It was a lot of "sound and fury signifying nothing." Hits aren't what matter; *conversions* are, that is, converting visitors to customers. And to do that, you have to be reaching *qualified prospects*.

But amid all that sound and fury, I got a fabulous Internet marketing education. With millions to spend, I had all the search engines flying people out to meet me, making me feel I was someone important. But of course, it wasn't about me at all; it was just about my budget. As a result, though, I got an amazing opportunity to learn all about the medium, including:

- The major search engine players
- Internet marketing products and offerings
- How to make advertising buys
- How to test results
- What was a good investment and what wasn't

Most important, I learned how to manage an Internet marketing strategy—what worked and what didn't.

I was laid off along with everyone else during the dot-com bust; but I gained a passion for figuring out a method of Internet marketing that would produce consistent results.

Paid search and keyword marketing were just coming online by then. I knew they would be extremely valuable and eventually would be the key to successful Internet marketing. I was introduced to Google™ AdWords and Yahoo!® Search Marketing®, and delved into how their programs worked. I learned that if you chose the right keywords and put some money behind those keywords, you could get consistent results.

Granted, it was a different world from what it is now. I had the personal phone number of someone at Yahoo! named Cindy. I could pick up the phone and call her if I had a question or need. Ah, the good old days!

Fast forward to July 2000, when I started Lutze Consulting in response to all the web site owners who had paid big money for web sites that weren't performing. I thought that if I heard, "If you build it, they will come" one more time, I was going to scream—mostly because it wasn't true. People didn't automatically come; you had to figure out how to get them to the site.

I became an expert at paid search techniques that worked. Over the past nine years and hundreds of clients, Lutze Consulting has excelled at Yahoo! Google, and MSN® visibility through optimization and paid search campaigns that work. I also became an expert at listening to frustrated business owners whose Internet marketing campaigns weren't working despite the money they were pouring into them. During this time, I also had the privilege of being one of three trainers hired to lead the Yahoo! Search Marketing Workshops for Success in 2006 and 2007. After training thousands of advertisers across the country, I gained a unique insight into the needs and frustrations of individual advertisers and business owners trying to manage their own search marketing campaigns.

In fact, I did a lot of listening. What I heard was that my clients and attendees were tired of wasting money on expensive traditional marketing and on failed Internet advertising. They wanted something new and fresh that would convert to qualified leads, actions, and purchases on their web sites.

Internet marketing *can* be that medium; but it requires a skilled and carefully crafted approach. Here is what I know from years of experience:

What works in the field of successful Internet marketing is keyword-driven searches.

I believe in keyword-driven searches because with this approach, **users qualify themselves.** They tell you (through their use of keywords) what they want. Then all you have to do is give it to them in the right way at the right time.

I believe in keyword-driven searches because they are trackable, from the first click to the final buy.

I believe in keyword-driven searches because, quite simply, they work.

And if you follow the approach recommended by this book, I'm confident that you'll become a believer, too.

CHAPTER 1

The Basics

The Long and Short of It

The Findability Formula is a search marketing guide for driving prospective customers to your site and delivering a user experience that converts those prospects into customers.

The formula has been crafted around two proven fundamental principles:

1. The secret to Internet marketing success is using the *right keywords* at the *right time* so that searchers can easily find you,

    That is what we call *findability*.

2. You must also appropriately *connect* with your prospects at all times by providing a *relevant result* in response to their search,

    That is what we call *delivering a good user experience*.

1

The second principle, though often overlooked, is as important as the first. You can't just focus on being "found" and "ranked" by the search engines because *customers*—not the search engines—are your target audience. Properly focusing on your *customers'* wants and needs gets you results in terms of sales *and* search engine rankings. That's why these two principles *working together* are the secret to Internet success.

This approach lets customers win because they are getting what they want and need; it lets search engines win because they are in the business of delivering good results to searchers; and it lets *you* win, because you've cracked the findability code and are showing up with good rankings in Internet searches on relevant pages relating to your product or service. This is the "sweet spot" where searchers are converted to **buyers.** It not only improves your bottom line by generating sales, it also improves your search engine rankings.

Improved ranking means better placement on a results page, which in turn usually means more site visitors; *further* improve your visibility, and therefore, your sales. It is a perfect circle of success breeding success. Additionally, as your paid ads begin to attract more clicks, you can actually end up paying less for them.

Let's move on to defining some of the terms we'll be using throughout the book.

Definitions

Findability

What is findability?

Wikipedia's definition of *findability* is spot-on in relation to search marketing. *Wikipedia* defines **findability as the quality of**

being locatable or navigable; and this is exactly what you're after in the realm of search marketing.

Sometimes people confuse *findability* with *branding,* and they're two different things. The goal of *branding* is to get something (company, name, product, service) *known.* It's about name recognition and is an effort to penetrate or saturate a given market space by getting a name, tagline, or logo out there. Branding doesn't require any action, response, or feedback from the customer. In that way, it might be considered a *passive* marketing approach.

Findability is an *active* process. It requires action on the part of the company to **make itself findable** and it requires an act on the part of the customer—first by initiating a search, and then by clicking on an ad or a search result.

Findability on the web means:

Findability

Findability refers to the quality of being locatable or navigable.

At the item level, we can evaluate to what degree a particular object is easy to discover or locate. At the system level, we can analyze how well a physical or digital environment supports navigation and retrieval.

Findability is not limited to the World Wide Web. The concept of findability is universal and timeless. However, with a distributed, heterogeneous collection of several billion items, the Web does present unique and important findability challenges.

Source: Wikipedia, the free encyclopedia.

You know how and when to appear on the *first page* of search engine results under the right *keywords* at the right time.

This book can guide you in that process.

Keywords

A keyword is *any word or series of words* (also known as keyphrases) entered into a search box on a search engine. This term can be confusing to members of the search marketing industry, because it's used in that field to mean either a single keyword (i.e. TV) and/or a keyword phrase (big screen TV) and/or a keyword string/search string (big screen plasma TV Denver). We call all these terms keywords because in the world of search engine marketing, **a keyword is simply any term a searcher types into a search box.** Whatever people type into a search box is called a keyword—even if it's more than one word. When searchers use a long string of words in their search, we sometimes refer to the keyword as a **keyword string** or a **long tail keyword** or a **long tail search term,** or a **search string,** and we generically refer to any search term as a keyword.

Keywords are the starting point for every prospect or customer when performing a search or making a purchase online. They are how your customers navigate the search process and how the search engines deliver results pages to searchers.

Search Engines

Search engines are the aggregators and classifiers of all the information available on the web. While at one time you might have visited a library and asked the librarian for information, today's "librarians" on the World Wide Web are the search engines. Instead of asking the librarian where you might find information on, say, Yugoslavia and having her direct you to those resources, now you type in *Yugoslavia,* and the search engines respond with links to the resources on that topic available on the web. We call the search engines' response to your query *search results, search engine results,* or just plain *results.*

Search Engine Results

There are two different groups of results: *sponsored* **results,** which is a term for results that an advertiser paid to show up on that page (through a paid search campaign); and there are *organic* **results,** which means the entry is there by virtue of the relevance of its web content and the repetition of certain keywords on its web pages. Getting your web site to show up in those results—and preferably on *the first page of those results*—is the science of search engine marketing.

Search Engine Marketing

Search Engine Marketing (also called **SEM** and *search marketing*) refers to marketing activities designed to increase the visibility or *findability* of a company, product, service, activity, organization or web site in search engine results. The two common methods of search marketing are *paid search* and *search engine optimization.*

Paid Search

Paid search is sometimes referred to as **pay per click (PPC),** or **cost per click (CPC).** With paid search, an advertiser is paying the search engines to display its ad on a particular search result page. Each time a searcher clicks on that ad, the search engine charges the advertiser's account a certain amount for each click.

PPC is the most common term people use when they're talking about paid search marketing. When they're running ads or groups of ads, they refer to them as **PPC campaigns.**

A PPC campaign is conducted by signing up with a search engine for a PPC advertising account. The PPC programs with the three major search engines (Google, Yahoo! and MSN) are called Google AdWords, Yahoo! Search Marketing, and Microsoft® adCenter. For ease of use throughout this book, we usually just call the programs Google, Yahoo! and MSN.

In contrast to *natural* or *organic* search results—in which the search engines control your placement on a given page—paid search allows a search engine marketer a fair amount of control over when and where to appear in response to a search result. However, like any advertiser in any medium, you pay for that privilege.

Natural Search

Natural search results are the results that the search engines determine are the most relevant response to a keyword that a user has typed in. People refer to these results as **natural, organic,** and **free** because you do not and cannot pay to be included there. Natural results and PPC ads both show up on results pages, and they appear in different locations on the page.

Search Engine Optimization

Search Engine Optimization, most commonly called **SEO**, is the way in which a search marketer attempts to influence the search engines in making their determinations about what constitutes a relevant result for a search. When people refer to SEO, they are talking about the manipulation of content to improve the chances that the search engines will recognize a web site or web page as a pertinent result—and their tendency to include it on a result page.

The "optimization" part is a strategy that involves organizing your site a certain way. It requires that you write your content in a way that optimizes your chances of the search engine finding you and giving you a good position under the search terms where you want to be found.

No matter how carefully you optimize your site for the search engines, you do not have control over whether, where, when, and how you appear on any given results page under any given keyword. That is controlled by the search engines—not by you. No matter how well you optimize your site, where and how you appear is almost completely up to the search engines. You can repeat certain keywords in your content so that the search engines recognize that search term as a good result; however, placement still rests with the search engines and the public is not privy to the intricate algorithms by which they make their determinations.

Achieving and maintaining high rankings in organic search results is a long-term and iterative process. Because of this, SEO is considered a more strategic approach to search marketing, whereas paid search is considered tactical.

Organic and PPC Placement

What people call *free listings* or *organic results* usually appear in the main and center section on search results pages and are displayed as "Search Results." Paid ads appear under and are called **Sponsored Links** in Google, **Sponsored Results** in Yahoo! and **Sponsored Sites** in MSN. Figure 1.1 is an example of a search results page, showing PPC ads and organic results. This page is from Google.

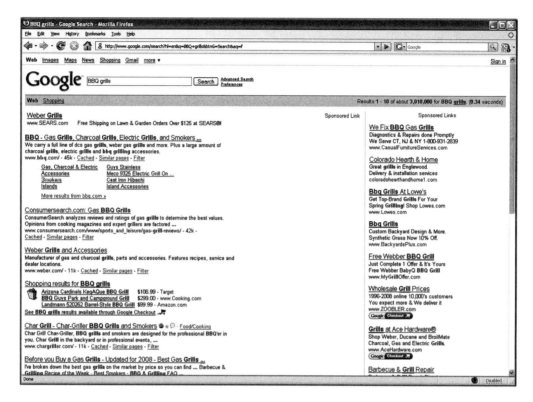

Figure 1.1   **Google Search Results Page**

Google screenshots © Google Inc. Used with permission.

In this example, the ads at the top and along the side are PPC or paid search ads, and the ads in the middle are natural or organic results. The location of the paid search ads can change from search engine to search engine, from keyword to keyword, and from page to page based on what the search engines determine will make them the most money.

Debunking the Free Myth

When it comes to competitive keywords, there is very little that is *free*, *organic*, or *natural* in the *free*, *organic*, *natural* listings that show up on Page One of search engine results. To show up under "natural" results on the first page, those sites have been *deliberately* optimized in almost all cases. The only way those spots could be considered free is that Google, Yahoo! and MSN are not charging every time someone clicks on them.

If a company appears on the first page of a popular keyword, it has almost certainly invested money in getting there. It has probably hired an SEO company and a skilled SEO writer to get that position. Its web pages have likely been carefully planned and designed to position the site on that page.

There's nothing free and little organic here. Page One placement is a result of skilled and careful manipulation. So, let's not call those results free or organic. Let's remove those terms from our vocabulary and refer to them instead as "SEO results"; because those listings have been deliberately optimized, probably at a cost, to get those positions.

Page One Visibility

The goal of both PPC and SEO findability is to show up on **the first page of the results,** whether we're talking about paid search or organic search. If you end up on page 63—or even on page 3—chances are no one is going to see you. In other words, you're not very findable.

Think about your own search habits. How often do you go past the first page when looking at results? You're not alone. According to a study by thinkeyetrack.com (http://thinkeyetracking.com/wordpress/?p=4), 87 percent of searchers studied do not bother to look beyond the first page of search results. Instead, they modify their search terms to get better results.

Page One is prime real estate in search engine marketing. It follows the same principle as traditional real estate: it's all about *location, location, location.* As an advertiser or business owner, the power of this space can make or break your business.

So, basically, you have one page—consisting of approximately 10 organic ("natural" or unpaid) listings and from 1 to 11 paid listings—to capture a customer. That's your window of opportunity for findability. Occasionally, two pages will do the trick; certainly no more than three is feasible. Your best shot is definitely Page One. *Findability is about showing up prominently on this page under your key search terms.*

Advertiser

When we use the term **advertiser,** we are talking about the person or company conducting a paid search campaign on the Internet. You are an "advertiser" once you have signed up with one of the search engines and have activated a PPC account.

Ad

Ad is the industry term for paid search engine entries on a results page. They don't really look like ads; they look like Figure 1.2.

Free Webber **BBQ Grill**
Just Complete 1 Offer & It's Yours
Free Webber BabyQ **BBQ Grill**
www.MyGrillOffer.com

Figure 1.2   **Example of a PPC Ad**
Google screenshots © Google Inc. Used with permission.

Customer

We use the word "customer" to refer to anyone who performs a search in a search engine and whom you want to find your business. Learning how to properly court and "convert" your customers—through the use of keywords—is the key to search marketing success.

Conversions

The whole point of search engine marketing is for you to get new customers, not *visitors* (i.e., window shoppers). *Customers* are people who take the **desired action** on your site. Usually that means **buying** something, but not always. It could mean signing up for a newsletter, downloading a white paper, registering for a class. Whatever you want someone who visits your site to **do,** if the visitor does it, that's called a *conversion*—you have succeeded in "converting" the visitor to a customer.

People lose sight of this all the time. They forget that conversions are the goal of marketing your business on the Internet. Not site visitors. Not "clicks." *Conversions.* Translation: CUSTOMERS!

Search Engines—The Big Three

When we talk about search engines in this book, we are usually referring to Google, Yahoo! and MSN. These are collectively known as the Big Three search engines simply because they are the three most commonly used search engines. In Figure 1.3, you can see the relative standing of the Big Three and why we focus on them.

The bottom line is that your goal is Page One visibility under your most important keywords in all three of these search engines.

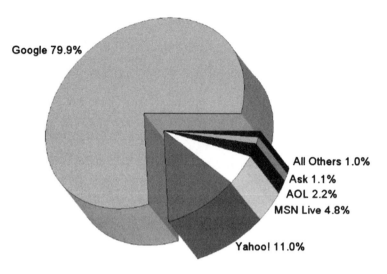

Google 79.9%

All Others 1.0%
Ask 1.1%
AOL 2.2%
MSN Live 4.8%

Yahoo! 11.0%

Figure 1.3   Search Engine Market Share

Source: http://www.marketshare.com.

Take-Aways

- The Findability Formula is a combination of using *the right keywords* so searchers can *find* you, and using them at *the right time* so searchers feel you are appropriately *connecting* with them. This delivers the optimal user experience.
- For search marketing success it is as important—if not more important—to focus on your *customers,* than to focus on the search engines.
- Focusing on customers and providing a good user experience is what converts *searchers* to *buyers.*
- The term "keyword" refers to a word or multiple words entered into a search box. *Big Screen Plasma TV* is a keyword.
- Search engine marketing (SEM) encompasses both pay per click (PPC) and search engine optimization (SEO).

- It is a myth that SEO is free. Rather, it typically requires a great deal of time or money and effort.
- Page One of search results is the only real estate that matters.
- The goal of search marketing isn't traffic, it's *conversions*— having the searcher take the desired action on your page.

Tools You Use in This Chapter
- *Wikipeida,* http://www.wikipedia.com

CHAPTER 2

First Things First

The concept of *findability* applies to both pay per click (PPC) and search engine optimization (SEO), and then to how they work together.

To be successful at SEO, *you must know your top-performing keywords.* You have to learn the keywords that work best for each company, and *paid search is the best way to learn what works and what converts.*

That is why we undertake PPC campaigns before SEO.

Everyone wants to start with SEO because they think it's *free;* however, to successfully optimize a web site, you need to know the keywords you want to optimize. Once you find the right keywords through PPC, you can begin an SEO effort. We begin with **paid search campaigns** because paid search gives us **hard data** about the keywords that will **perform** best.

Paid search (PPC) also:

- Gets up and running quickly
- Is trackable and quantifiable
- Provides instant search engine recognition
- Allows spending to be precise and controllable
- Enables easy testing and tracking of keywords and conversions
- Provides specific and instant feedback
- Ensures your listing will be on the first page (which SEO does not)

In contrast, **SEO:**

- Is *not* guaranteed.
- Is *not* "free." It requires a significant amount of time and energy, and usually money (time is also money).
- Is a three- to six-month project, minimum. Most businesses—and especially new businesses—can't wait six months, or however long it may take, to start appearing in organic search results.
- Involves making researched, detailed changes to your web site.
- Is a moving target. The algorithms (intricate and complicated secret formulas) used by the search engines change over time. When the search engines update their algorithms, your ranking can change instantly and you can fall off first-page results.
- If others optimize their site better, they will rank higher than you and can bump your position.
- SEO includes unknown factors that the search engines don't share with the public.

Once you know your core converting keywords from which your customers *buy* (your "money keywords"), *then* you will want to start on SEO. Remember, SEO remains a moving target, not an exact science. Even when you know your keywords, SEO doesn't produce consistent and reliable placement, whereas paid search is dependable, repeatable, and *reliable.*

Paid search is the perfect arena to start and test your keywords, and it's where you learn exactly which keywords customers are purchasing from. Often, it is not the words you might guess.

Naysayers on the subject of paid search like to imply that users prefer natural search results and avoid the paid ads. That is simply not true. Statistics show that users don't differentiate between paid and SEO entries. They scan for *relevance.*

The bottom line is this: Page One placement under *the right keywords* can generate significant revenue for your business—and paid search is the first step in getting there.

Conducting Your Paid Search Campaign

The findability formula provides fundamentals and acts as a guide for undertaking a successful paid search campaign.

It will save you significant amounts of money, time, and frustration because it requires you to stop and think about these questions before you start an advertising campaign:

- Who are your prospects or customers?
- How are they going to search for your product or service?
- How are they going to find you in the search engines?
- What do you need to give users at every stage in their search process to get them to say "yes" to you?

Knowledge before Action

This book covers the fundamentals and practical steps for the deployment of a paid search campaign. It also explains how paid search translates to a productive, organic, SEO-friendly keyword strategy.

Whether your primary interest is PPC or SEO—and no matter whether you're going to undertake a search marketing campaign yourself or hire an agency to do it—reading this book will be of enormous benefit in understanding the steps to successful search marketing and protecting yourself from costly mistakes.

One of the reasons you need to understand the fundamentals of search marketing is that people sometimes forget that the search engines are in the business of making money. They're not just altruistic "keepers" of the content; they have their own best interests at heart (as well they should), and you need to look out for your own best interests to become visible and findable on the Internet. The more you learn about search marketing and the PPC process—and how the interests of your business goals, the search engines and your customers can work in productive alignment—the better.

The P Words

In most cases, for your company to be easily found on the Internet, you have to have **Page One** visibility on the search results pages under the keywords most relevant to your business. And, in most cases—at least at the beginning of your search marketing efforts—you must be willing to *pay* for that visibility through a paid search campaign.

Figures 2.1 through 2.3 are examples of where PAID SEARCH ads show up on the three major search engines.

The most important thing to keep in mind about these ads is that this positioning costs you money. And if you're *paying for the positioning,* then you must be sure that you've chosen the *right keywords* to optimize your chances that the prospect clicking on your ad will turn into a *paying* customer.

Finding out those keywords and using them to your advantage represent what we call the *art of the keyword.* This is an art with a solid methodology behind it, so maybe we should have called it the *science of the keyword.* In any case, here's how it works.

Let's say I've just finished a book about paid search marketing and I want it to appear in the search results for anyone

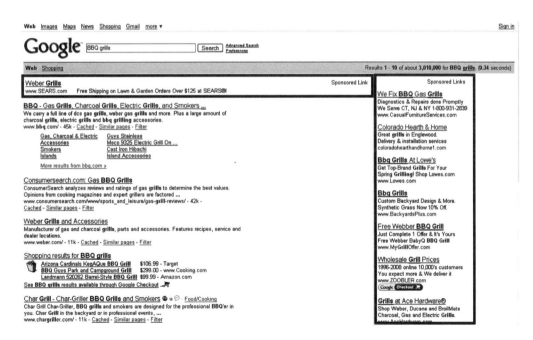

Figure 2.1   **Google Paid Search**

Google screenshots © Google Inc. Used with permission.

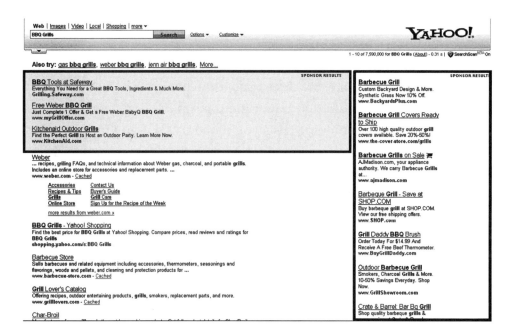

Figure 2.2 **Yahoo! Paid Search**

Yahoo! Screenshots. Used with permission.

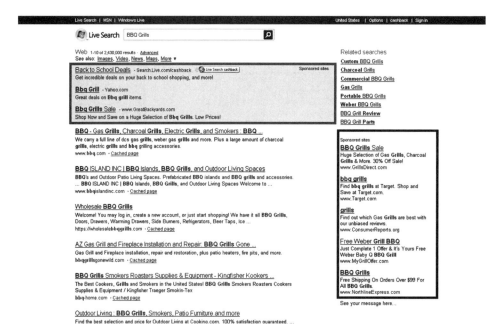

Figure 2.3 **MSN Paid Search**

MSN adCenter Screenshots. Used with permission.

looking on the Internet for a book about search engine marketing. To ensure my appearance on a top results page, I'm willing to pay for my ad to appear in the **sponsored search results.** However, since I am acutely aware that I'll be paying a fee every time someone clicks on my ad, I want to be absolutely sure that my book is what the searcher is looking for before that click. How will I do that?

By applying a *laser focus* to the keywords under which I choose to appear.

Laser Focus

If I were to pick *marketing book* as the keyword phrase for the page I want my ad to show up on, I'd probably be making a mistake. Yes, it's a marketing book; however, that's too broad a term to attract the customer for whose attention I am willing to **pay.**

Even the terms *Internet marketing* or *Internet sales* would be too broad and insufficiently targeted for the customer I'm after. The searchers that I want to click on my ad—the ad I'm paying for them to click on—are the *customers most likely to purchase the book.* I wouldn't even pick *Search Marketing* or *Pay Per Click Marketing* as my keyword phrase, because I still wouldn't know *exactly* what someone who is typing that into the search box is actually looking for. These terms may be related; however, they're not **precisely targeted** terms.

However, if I were to choose Paid Search Marketing Book or *Search Engine Marketing Book* as my keyword phrase, then I'm getting close to honing in on the specific intent of the person who typed in that search term. That searcher is presumably looking for a book about paid search marketing; in that case, I'm more than willing to have him or her click on my ad because there's an excellent likelihood that a book purchase will result.

How do I know that? The search term tells me—because

Keywords are what broadcast the searcher's intent.

By choosing to appear under those specific keyword searches, the odds are pretty good that I'm getting in front of a *qualified, interested,* prospective customer.

Chapter 4—The Art of the Keyword will walk you through choosing your own keywords, and it's important to understand here that honing in on the right keywords—not just *targeting*, **pinpointing** your customers by their (and your) keyword choices—is the way to paid search marketing success.

Try this: Stop reading for a minute, and go to your computer. Then go to www.google.com and type in "search engine marketing book" and see what happens. Depending on when you are reading this book—and how close that is to its publication date—what you should see is *The Findability Formula* ad in one of the top three positions in the Sponsored Results section of the page.

A Good Click

Now, I'm getting a little ahead of myself. I've devoted entire sections to writing ads and where the click should take a prospect to deliver a relevant user experience. Go ahead and click on the ad now anyway; because what happens next is important.

As an advertiser, you're not after just a *good click* for yourself because you're paying for that customer. You also want the customer to have a *good click* experience.

When you click on the ad for *The Findability Formula,* you'll notice that rather than being taken to my web site's home page (a common error) you'll be delivered to the page on my site that is *about the book.* So, when customers arrive at the "after the click" destination, they won't feel frustrated or confused. They won't be annoyed that they clicked on something about a search marketing book and end up on some consulting site. They'll be right on the page they wanted that has the very information they were seeking.

Avoiding Bad Clicks

We've all had bad click experiences on the search engines when our hunt for a particular topic has resulted in a page full of unrelated results. It's annoying. What you *and* your customer *and* the search engines are after is a **good search experience** with a **super-relevant search result.** It should be satisfying for the advertiser, the searcher, and the search engine alike. Most importantly, it's what generates *sales* and a good return on your paid search investment.

The search engines reward good results, because this builds their credibility. They want the pages they give to searchers to be as relevant as possible, and they reward advertisers who pay attention to this with a better "quality score" (see Chapter 11—After the Click) that improves your ad placement and rates.

One of the ways we deliver a good search result to users is by understanding how people actually use the Internet to search for products and services, and by responding appropriately to them in their search process. This, quite conveniently, is the subject of Chapter 3—How People Search, Shop, and Buy Online.

Take-Aways

- When developing your search marketing campaign, you might want to try PPC before SEO so you can determine which search terms are your best converting keywords and apply them to your SEO efforts.
- PPC produces results more quickly and more reliably than SEO.
- When you know your performing keywords you can apply them to your SEO campaign.
- When someone clicks on a PPC ad, it is critical to take them to completely relevant information for the search term they typed in.

Tools You Use in This Chapter
- Google, http://www.google.com
- Yahoo!, http://www.yahoo.com
- MSN, http://www.msn.com

CHAPTER 3

How People Search, Shop, and Buy Online

Path to Purchase

Pay per click (PPC) and search engine optimization (SEO) are complex processes. Achieving success in either arena requires an understanding of your customers' behavior and the search terms they use to find your product or service all along their "path to purchase."

Correcting a Common Misconception

A common mistake advertisers make is failing to understand how people use the Internet to purchase products or services. A business owner's dream would be for a searcher to type in a keyword, click on their ad in the search results, go to their home page, find the product, and buy right then and there.

However, that isn't how it works.

Online purchasing is a *process* that involves numerous actions over a period of time. It's a *path* with a beginning, middle, and an end. And here's how it goes: The customer has a problem, desire, need or some form of discomfort. We will call this the customer's *pain factor*. Let's say that your TV wouldn't work this morning. The broken TV is your pain factor.

If you turn to the Internet to solve your problem, you are probably not going to purchase a new TV online *today*. Online purchases rarely take place in one visit with one search. It is a process that usually involves customers returning to the Internet multiple times before making a purchase. They go through a *buying cycle*—a sequence of behaviors—before making a decision to buy.

Through a *series of searches,* someone with a broken TV will start the *process* of deciding to either repair the TV or buy a new one. (Both of these are considered purchases; in one case, it's a service purchase and in the other it's a product purchase.) This *series of searches* or *process* is called the **path to purchase.**

The Buying Cycle

In the world of the Internet, the buying cycle happens in three general phases:

1. **Information:** Researching and gathering data
2. **Shopping:** Comparing and contrasting brands, features, benefits, and advantages
3. **Purchasing:** Comparing price, locations, product model numbers, and other specific criteria

---

At each phase of the journey, customers use different keywords to get more and more relevant results in response to what they're searching for.

Usually, they add more and more descriptions, qualifiers, and modifiers as they get a better idea of what they want and move increasingly closer to purchasing or taking action.

Because of that, a successful search engine marketer needs to understand the answer to this question above all else:

What keywords will my customers be using—and when—along their path to purchase?

More specifically:

- What are the general "pain factors" that my product or service addresses?
- What do my customers type into the search box when they're looking for information on my product/service?
- What do they type in as they're narrowing their search and honing in on what they want?
- What are the keywords they're using when their credit cards are out and they're ready to buy?

The Keyword Trail

The answers to these questions give us a path that we call the **keyword trail.** Understanding *the keyword trail* ensures that you stay with your customers throughout their journey, particularly when they are finally **ready to buy.**

The next step is to find out what keywords customers are using as they search for your product/service. And that's the **art of the keyword.**

Take-Aways

- Online purchasing is a *process*. It is not a one-time event. There is a path to purchasing online.
- The path to purchase follows a three-phase buying cycle that includes *information gathering*, *shopping*, and *taking a desired action*, that is, *purchase or lead generation*.
- Searchers may use different keywords at each phase of the process.
- The keywords tend to get longer and more specific as searchers get closer to taking action.

CHAPTER 4

The Art of the Keyword

Why Keywords Are Key

If the eyes are the windows to the soul, the keyword search is the window to your customer's thinking process. Understanding the way prospects and customers utilize keywords on their path to making a purchase is the greatest challenge and also the greatest reward in the world of Search Engine Marketing (SEM).

Developing and refining keywords is an ongoing and iterative process that is never finished. There will always be newer and better and more targeted keywords for you to find. You can *start on the right track,* which most companies—believe it or not—do not.

Leaving the Laundry

Those advertisers who are new to paid search hope that their ad campaigns will be the make-or-break solution to their business. Most of them set up their paid search accounts by dumping a bunch of high-level, generic keywords onto their campaigns, writing a few uninspired ads, and then turning on their pay per click account with all ads going to the company's home page.

When that strategy doesn't produce satisfactory results, these advertisers get upset or become convinced that paid search marketing doesn't work. Then they start calling Google and Yahoo! and MSN a bunch of crooks and questioning the value and validity of paid search. They think it's a total waste of time and money, and they're angry about the resources that they've dumped into it. And now they're convinced that paid search marketing is worthless and undeserving of any investment at all.

Every search marketing consultant has seen businesses—from small mom-and-pops all the way to multimillion-dollar companies—go through this cycle when their paid search campaigns fail to perform for them. It happens because these advertisers put as much effort into their campaigns as throwing in a load of laundry, pushing "start," and walking away. They're unhappy with results; and they never look at the total lack of preparation and effort they put in.

The next phase we see is these advertisers' efforts to redeem their accounts. Even if they spend more money, exhaust internal resources, and spend hours on the phone enduring hours of frustration with the technical support people at Google, Yahoo! and MSN—they *still* may not get the results they want.

And finally if they call in an agency to save them (thus making it the agency's responsibility to redeem the medium), disappointment may still ensue.

Why?

Because their campaigns have been set up with flawed basics; indeed, it's almost impossible for them *not* to fail.

Successful search engine marketing requires that you understand the fundamentals of the search process and the mindset of your prospects as well as how they use keywords to find you and that you come to realize how you should use keywords to reach them.

Narrowing the Field

Perhaps the ***most important part of the art of the keyword*** is what we call ***narrowing the field.*** Narrowing the field is about targeting your users and your keywords in a specific and results-oriented manner to the satisfaction of your customer, you (the advertiser) and your bottom line.

If you learn nothing else from this book, please learn this because the ***most successful PPC campaigns*** choose the right, highly targeted and specific keywords to get the desired results.

The example in Chapter 2—First Things First—about marketing this book via a Google search illustrates the importance of targeting your keywords to get worthwhile pay per click (PPC) results. Here's another example: If a business that sells televisions created a paid search campaign with the word *televisions* or *TVs* as its keyword—hoping for *sales*—that campaign will almost certainly fail. Why? Because those are the ***least-targeted keywords*** they could possibly choose. "Televisions" is a broad, generic, and *informational* keyword. It is being used at a very early stage in the buying cycle, and it is not a targeted sales term.

With a little effort and market knowledge, that advertiser would realize that people don't really buy "televisions"; their purchases are much more specific. People buy flat-screen televisions, or plasma televisions or rear-projection televisions. Maybe they want a state-of-the art-home theater, or a bargain-priced TV, or used TV or TV repair. Maybe they want to buy a Sony TV or a Panasonic or whatever . . . it's not just "TVs" that they're looking for when they're ready to buy.

It is too general a term for effective paid search results if the advertiser is hoping for sales.

We see this kind of mistake all the time in search marketing consulting. Angry, frustrated advertisers call us ranting that search engine marketing doesn't work and that it's a big waste of money. "I spent all this money on Internet advertising," they tell us, "and I didn't get any results." They're upset—and who could blame them?

Their dismal results are the consequence of blowing their budget on a keyword that is *informational* rather than *purchasing* oriented. The campaign was bound to fail if they were hoping for *sales.*

For some companies, money is no object; and they're willing to dump an endless amount of funds into search marketing campaigns based on the law of averages. They trust that eventually they'll get at least *some* customers and some measure of success, even by using broad, generic terms. Frankly, that's a foolhardy approach for most businesses.

A better way of operating is to understand that not only are there the *right* keywords for your business, that within that group, there are *informational* keywords, *shopping* keywords, and *purchasing* keywords with appropriate and effective applications for each category.

Secret Sauce

Understanding your customer's path to purchase and providing the right keywords is based on a **series of ingredients** that need to be added at the right time, in the right way, for a valuable end result.

The keyword is the crucial ingredient that makes everything come together in just the right way to produce the special "secret sauce" that spells success.

The task at hand is figuring out how to identify the path, the keyword string, and what you should be giving customers at each step (as they keep adding variables to their search).

Every person who is marketing a product or service on the Internet has to navigate through this challenge. The path to the most productive and highest-converting ad campaigns leading to a high percentage of customer purchases is carved through **the keyword experience.**

Your customers' keyword searches and clicks are the signposts. Their search terms will clearly tell you what they want at each stage of their search query and what keywords you should use and what you should give them to address their intention and desire. ***Aligning the correct keywords with the searcher's intent*** is the essential ingredient for a successful search campaign.

They'll tell you what their intent is; and you need to learn to read the signs.

Take-Aways

- Choosing the right keywords is the most important part of a successful search marketing campaign.
- Highly targeted and specific keywords get the best *sales* results and are far more effective than broad non-specific terms.
- Searchers broadcast their desires and intent through their choice of keywords.
- Successful search marketing lies in understanding what a searcher wants (through the use of keywords) and delivering a keyword-relevant user experience.

CHAPTER 5

Keyword Alignment on the Path to Purchase

To choose and use the right keywords at the right time in your pay per click (PPC) campaigns, you must be clear about the customers' intent at each stage of the buying cycle and their search. You can determine this largely by what the customers are communicating to you through the search terms they're using and the number of words (length) of the search string.

Keyword Tails and Search Strings

A search string or keyword phrase is more than one word in a search query. The level of satisfaction a search delivers is almost always determined by the search string, and often by the number of words in the string.

Step into your prospects' shoes for a moment, and imagine how they might begin a search. Start with a very basic search term and view the results in a search engine. Then add another term onto your search string. Are you satisfied yet? Probably not, so add more terms. How about now? Did you get the result you needed or wanted?

This is the same process your customers go through every time they search. They keep adding keywords onto their search query to get better and better results.

The process of adding keywords to a general initial search term until a valuable or relevant search result is found is called a **keyword tail.** Your prospects might start with the word *television* or *TV,* and end up with a page of not-very-useful results; or at least, not what they are looking for. This frustrates users, so they keep entering additional modifiers. They make the keyword phrases longer and longer until they get the results that satisfy their search intent.

Searchers want to get the most valuable search results with the least amount of work. They don't want to dig in page after page until they find the result they are looking for. They want a relevant result as quickly as possible, and that's what the search engines attempt to deliver. Longer keyword phrases are requests for more specific information, and that's what the search engines will give them.

Let's say John Smith of Dayton, Ohio, has a broken television on the Friday before the big game. His TV is too big to fit in his car, and he is freaking out! You can probably feel his pain.

John turns to the Internet to find a possible solution to his problem. He's likely to start by using the search term *televisions.* However, this will probably not address his pain and his particular issue. He will then incrementally add keywords that get him closer

Table 5.1   **Path to Purchase**

Keyword	Results Size	Cost Per Click	User Experience Rating
Televisions	435,000,000	$$$$	☹
Television Repair	983,000	$$$	☺
Television Repair Sony	434,000	$$	☺☺
Television Repair Sony Dayton	65,100	$	☺☺☺
Television Repair Sony Dayton OH	45,000	$	☺☺☺☺+
Television Repair Sony Dayton OH On Site Repair	5,940	$	☺☺☺☺+

to easing his pain and solving his problem. Table 5.1 maps John's "path to purchase."

This example shows that unless someone is seeking broad information, broad (generic) terms tend to deliver less satisfying results. So they will keep adding search terms, getting fewer and more targeted results.

In the end, *Television Repair Sony Dayton OH on site repair* has given John Smith a satisfying result. He has found what he was looking for all along. And if the ad that he clicks on mentions his concerns and then takes him to a relevant page with the information he is seeking, then that repair shop is likely to get John's business—*especially* if the page mentions hours, weekend, and evening availability; specifically tells the customer if you need us, "we will come to you"; and perhaps includes estimated service call prices. That's a completely satisfying user experience. John's pain has been addressed and he's going to pick up the phone and make that call. Mission accomplished . . . for the business, the customer, and the search engine.

The path to purchase doesn't usually take place quite so quickly. These stages typically occur over time, instead of in one sitting. We're just using John Smith's situation to show how searchers add terms in an iterative process until they get what they're looking for.

There are times when broad, informational terms are entirely appropriate. There are searchers typing in the generic term "mountain bikes" because they want general information about mountain bikes—brands, features, prices, and comparisons. And if they're using that term and staying on that page, then you want to deliver what they're asking for. And they're not typing in "mountain bikes" when they're ready to buy one. They're typing in a much longer keyword with lots of specifics.

No matter where the searcher is in the search process, you want to target the terms you use and the results you deliver. And if you're after buyers, you're going to want to target your keywords with long search strings and lots of details.

Advantages of Targeting Your Keywords

There are three top advantages to targeting your keywords.

1. It awards searchers a satisfying user experience, which increases your chances of a conversion.
2. The search engines appreciate and reward advertisers who deliver relevant results and good user experiences with perks such as:
   — Better placement on search results pages
   — Lower costs for you when bidding on your search terms

3. Exact targeted keywords (because they generate less traffic) generally cost *less* than generic, broader keywords (because they generate higher traffic). You might think that the opposite is true since the narrower terms are the more converting terms, and that's not how it goes. People pay higher prices for the terms that will bring them more traffic. So, terms like *televisions* or *mountain bikes* generally cost more than longer keywords. Ergo, you are doing yourself a favor with more targeted terms in two ways:

1. You're generally paying less for your keywords.
2. You're getting in front of *purchasers,* not window shoppers.

And you can't just randomly elongate your keywords and hope for better results. The keywords—and what you deliver in response to them—have to be *correlated* to the appropriate buying cycle phase.

Phased Searches

The various stages of the buying cycle prompt different kinds of consumer searches. During the **information** phase, the search query usually involves one- or two-word generic information terms. The **shopping** cycle usually involves two to three still generic words. And during the **buying** phase, consumers are likely to use four-word or longer keywords with less generic terms that include brand names and detailed specifications. When the customer is typing in more and more keywords that include specific search terms, that's when the wallet is in hand and the person is ready to buy.

So, by the time customers are entering terms such as *LG French Door Refrigerator Cleveland OH* into a search box, they're getting close to buying. At that point in their search, you have to give them a *very specific* response or you will lose them. However, if you're too detailed, specific, or brand-centric too early in the process—when all that your customer is doing is research or comparison shopping—then that's a mismatch as well.

This can be a difficult balance to strike. If the user is searching for *refrigerators* in the early stage of information gathering and you immediately send that searcher to your shopping cart, then the person is likely to be frustrated and will probably hit the "back" button to review the other sites offered on the results page. If, the keyword typed in is *LG French Door Refrigerator Cleveland OH* and the result is a generic "refrigerators" page, frustration will also ensue. The information and shopping phases are over with; this user is ready to buy, and you're not delivering an appropriate result.

This is why it is critical that you understand the phases of the path to purchase, and what customers want at each phase.

Information Phase

Step 1 in the buying cycle is **information gathering.** During this stage, the customers don't yet know what they want. They are only aware that there is a pain, a problem, a need, or desire that they're trying to solve or meet. It is similar to customers driving around the outside of a mall, not even sure what stores they might go into.

Your broadest terms—the most generic keywords—are your **informational keywords.** These are also the shortest search terms, usually only one or two words, like "television." What you provide the searcher with at the keyword "television" and what you display when they type in a longer keyword string *Sony 24 inch flat screen* should be two different things. You must always keep in mind the desire and intent that *the searchers' terms reveal*. A customer who types "televisions" into the search box is in the information and research gathering stage. That customer is not ready to buy; the credit card is still in a wallet that hasn't yet been taken out.

There is no scientific way of telling how long the information gathering stage will last. It differs significantly among different products and services. The general guidelines are that ***the higher the price point, the longer the information stage.*** A customer looking for a $2.00 widget will usually move through information gathering rather quickly, whereas someone researching $2,000.00 televisions will have a much longer information-gathering and decision-making stage.

One-off business to consumer (B2C) items (e.g., books and CDs) and items priced at under $100, tend to have a short sales cycle. Business to business (B2B) products and services have much longer sales cycles, are more relationship-based, and often require a more complex education process that may involve webinars, conversations with sales reps, and mailing of informational materials. As an advertiser, it is important for you to understand your particular market, and your customers' specific buying cycle by asking the following questions:

- Is your product or service simple or complex?
- Is the decision-making process usually short or long?
- What is the normal sales process for your specific product or service?

Once you know the process for your market niche, you can begin to think about which keywords apply to which phase, and how to structure a PPC ad campaign with informational, shopping, and buying keywords in their proper sequence.

Although broad informational terms are usually associated with the first phase of a path to purchase, there are some exceptions. If your product or service is information (e.g., *Consumer Reports*, or research/comparison studies, definitions, or explanations) then informational terms might be appropriate for every campaign. You would be providing a good user experience at every point, because the user is searching for information all along the path.

Generic keywords and broad terms are also useful if your goal is *branding* your business. In that case, you might *want* your company name to come up on any and every television-related search—targeted or generic because you're not seeking sales; you're trying to make a name for yourself in the TV market. In such a situation, generic or informational terms have a purpose, because you set them up in their own campaign called a "branding" campaign, and you assign a special budget for these "awareness" terms. If you're after sales, however, then you must understand all three phases of the buying cycle and how keywords play in to each.

Shopping Phase

Once customers have moved past the research stage, they begin **shopping:** looking at and comparing features, sizes, colors, brand names, price points, and retailers. This shows up in the world of on-line purchasing as customers putting more words onto their search terms, or "keyword tail." This is the phase where terms like *Sony Silver Flat Panel* and *Sony Plasma 37 inch* are showing up, and where customers are adding more modifiers onto their root search term and more specific keywords to get more detailed results. Longer and more specific search strings indicate that the customer is in hardcore shopping mode.

This would be the point in the brick-and-mortar world where shoppers have parked and entered the mall, and are walking in and out of several stores. They're looking at various options and narrowing down their choices as they go.

Only you know how long this phase generally lasts in your own business, and what is the most important information to deliver at this point. Search marketing considers the "shopping" phase as signaled by search terms two to three and maybe even four keywords in length.

Purchasing Phase

Purchasing keywords are the longest and most specific searches of all. Now the customer's search terms won't be general terms like televisions or even Sony Televisions and will be more like Sony 32 inch plasma in Denver Colorado. Terms like these indicate that the customer has stopped wandering around the mall and has made a decision. The person has walked into a specific store and is standing at the wall where all the 32 inch plasma televisions are on display, deciding which TV to purchase.

Your online customers indicate this purchasing readiness by the number of specific elements in their search terms. While there is no one term that will absolutely tell you they are ready to buy, you can make certain assumptions based on the length and specificity of the keyword phrase.

Purchasing Keywords

If you're spending money on a search marketing campaign to garner sales, then you're going to want to focus on *purchasing* keywords—the longer and more specific keyword phrases.

WARNING

Longer, more specific, highly targeted keyword phrases will have a lower search volume than general terms. That should not cause you . . . undue concern because their *conversion rate* will most likely be higher.

What exactly does that mean? That targeted purchasing keywords will put you in front of customers who know exactly what they want and who are *ready to buy.* When customers are typing in keywords like *television 32 inch Sony flat screen plasma Denver Colorado*, they have finished shopping; they have decided on what they're going to buy and in what geographic area.

If you go to the extra effort of running a long string, highly specific keyword in your campaign such as *television 32 inch Sony flat screen plasma Denver Colorado* you're going to be right there when the customer's credit card is coming out. Indeed, you might be one of a few search results on that page . . . maybe even the only one. The customer's response is "Wow, these guys understand exactly what I want and they have exactly what I want," and a sale becomes highly probable. So it should matter less to you that there will be fewer searches on this specific term (low search volume) if a high percentage of searchers become purchasers (high conversion rates). Would you rather have 10,000 searches and no conversions or 1,000 searches and 20 conversions?

Always keep in mind that you want **conversions**. You want to *convert* passive searchers to users and have them click on your ad; and then you want to convert a site visitor to take the action on your site required to become a purchaser. If your site isn't a retail site, visitors are considered "conversions" if you have gotten them to say "yes" to whatever action you want them to take on your site.

This might involve actions, and if what you were hoping for when you agreed to pay for them to click on your ad happens . . . then that's a conversion. It's your business; you know what a "yes" is for your company.

Table 5.2 shows the relationship between keyword length and search phase along the path to purchase.

Table 5.2   **How Customers Search—Implications**

	Learn→	Shop→	Purchase
Keyword length	One to two words	Two to three words	Four or longer words
Search volume	High	Medium	Low
Opportunity	Frame the buying decision	Compete on more specific criteria	Obtain a ready sale now
	Establish credibility	Capitalize on customer preferences	Acquire customers who know what they want
Conversion rate	Low	Medium	High

Courtesy of Mary O'Brien, President AlterAct Marketing and Chair of PPC Summits.

Establishing Trust

My clients all tend to ask me the same question after I've explained the buying cycle and the process of carefully targeting keywords for each stage in the cycle:

Since what I'm after is SALES, why wouldn't I just run campaigns with purchasing terms and focus only on getting in front of customers at the point they're ready to buy?

Good question. Here's the answer: sometimes you have to start building trust, authority, and name recognition with your customer early in the process. You can't just throw your hat into the ring at the last minute. Your competitors, especially the big guys, have been present all along. You can't insert yourself at the last stage of the game and be considered a contender unless you offer something totally unique or really phenomenal; and even under those circumstances, participating at the last minute is often not enough to close the sale.

Let's return to the *Sony 32 inch plasma TV*. A typical customer researches and shops for that product for a few days, comes to recognize the names that are prevalent in that space. Suddenly, at the last minute, your company's name appears in the results—and they've never heard of you before. What are your chances of turning this searcher into a customer?

If customers see your name or your ad multiple times along their path to purchase, you earn another checkmark or climb another notch in their authority and credibility index. If they've come across your information three or four times along their path—and perhaps even clicked on your site and received some useful information from you—they feel much better about purchasing from you; not only from a security standpoint, also in terms of reputation and trust. If you have been with them along their way, provided them what they asked for at various phases in their search, and responded to their needs, you've created a *relationship* with them.

Often advertisers who pay attention to this subtlety will win the customer. Customers who finally reach the purchasing point have seen the advertiser's name many times; that establishes a pretty good comfort level. Maybe there's even been a visit to the company's web site; maybe the site's been bookmarked. Whatever the reaction, this is an important step in helping your customers feel comfortable doing business with you. This is especially important with online purchases. When all other things—price, shipping, quality, ease of purchase—are equal, the tiebreaker will always be "Whom Can I Trust?" Keep this in mind when organizing your keyword campaigns. If you can afford more than just your purchasing terms, then don't just show up at the end of the search.

The End Game

With search marketing, you have at least two opportunities to be found for your keywords: PPC and SEO. Your *ultimate* goal is for searchers to find your company easily under carefully selected keywords that are relevant to your business at every stage in your customers' path to purchase. When searchers see your company listed in both the organic and paid listing, you double your exposure and your opportunity for them to click. This is how you win in search marketing.

That's how you get business from the Internet.

The Pause That Refreshes

If your campaign isn't performing, chances are that you haven't chosen the appropriate keywords and keyword phrases, and are not properly meeting your customers along their path to purchase.

In some ways, it's great that setting up a paid search account is so easy, and I sometimes worry that it's *too* easy. Anyone can just put keywords into the spreadsheet, set a budget, and activate an account. Anyone can do it, without a clue about what they're doing. And their company may well suffer by their doing so.

I suggest that you put any non-performing campaigns on pause. Trust me: every day that your campaigns are running without the proper keywords and campaign settings equals money being thrown away. Stop paying for all those useless clicks. Instead, read the rest of this book, make the recommended changes, and then reactivate your ad campaigns. It will make a world of difference in your campaign performance and your return on investment.

Take-Aways

- Searchers keep adding words to their initial search term to get better and more relevant results. This is called a "search string" or "keyword tail."
- To achieve maximum conversions, your keyword campaigns need to be as narrowly targeted as possible to align with searchers' specific search strings.
- Narrowly targeted, highly specific terms get better placement on a results page, cost less than broader, generic terms, and deliver better conversion rates. Highly targeted terms tend to get you in front of purchasers.
- It is important to understand the terms in your own industry that indicate the buying cycle of your customers and to deliver appropriate results to them at every phase along their path to purchase.

CHAPTER 6

The Keyword
Discovery Process

Impatience

If you're getting a little frustrated and impatient because we've
spent so much time laying a foundation for your search marketing
campaign, and we haven't actually had you *do* anything yet, fear
not; in this chapter, we have you do quite a bit. Your future Internet
marketing success is dependent on laying a strong foundation for
your advertising campaigns.

Anyone can dump a cluster of keywords into a paid search
account and turn the campaign on; that approach, however, almost always guarantees disappointment and lousy results. We're
trying to *avoid* that by having you understand exactly how search

marketing works when it's done properly, and then by having you go through the next steps. Experience teaches us that:

The first mistake people usually make with their paid search campaigns is rushing to get them up and running.

They want to take a bunch of what they consider to be "obvious" keywords, and get them up on the Internet and see what happens, however:

Your keywords will make or break your paid search campaign, so it is far better to take some time to find the keywords that will perform for you.

Understanding the process and then choosing your keywords carefully and wisely is a little slower at the front end; however, it pays off in spades later.

Finding Your Keywords

As business owners or account managers, it's easy for us to get caught up in our **core belief** or **ego** keywords. We're so certain we know the keywords in our own business that we sometimes fail to consider things from the *customers'* point of view. We are often too close to our own field and marketing materials to figure out how *customers* search for our products and services—especially the words that they use when they are ready to buy.

Company-Centric Keywords

A case in point is a recent search engine optimization project that I completed for a heating, ventilating, and air conditioning (HVAC) maintenance and repair company. The company was absolutely certain that its most important keyword was *HVAC* because that is how they thought of themselves and referred to them internally.

However, that's not what their customers typed in when their air conditioner or heat wasn't working. If you wake up seeing your breath in the middle of January in Boston, you search for *furnace repair* or *heating repair*—not HVAC. When this company's customers needed them, they typed *heating company Boston* or *heater repair Boston* into the search box. And on 97-degree days, customers wanted *air conditioner repairs* or *air conditioner sales*—not HVAC.

Step back from all your assumptions about what your keywords are and start fresh, using the keyword exercises in this chapter. No matter what you, your executives, your sales managers, or your board members think your keywords are, until you have made the effort to get into your *customers'* heads, you do not know for certain how they search or buy online.

I'm also going to encourage you to walk away from your ego keywords or the keywords under which you would love to see your name in the big engines. This isn't about how you'd like to be known or perceived, or about the keywords that would give you a "rush." Believe me—I've gone that route. I've spent money to be on results pages that did nice things for my self-image, however, didn't generate new users or cash flow. And they didn't do a thing for my business.

Mapping Out Your Keyword Strategy

Your keyword strategy consists of four steps:

1. Creating your positioning statement
2. Conducting a keyword brainstorming session
3. Using a keyword discovery tool
4. Identifying your negative keywords

When you've completed these four steps, you will have your keyword list.

Step 1: Your Positioning Statement

Soul Searching

We're going to start the keyword discovery process by asking you to do some soul searching about your business.

Do businesses even *have* souls? I think that they do. In fact, defining and expressing the soul of your business is a key element of marketing yourself on the Internet.

Before you start to focus on your keywords, you need to think in some fairly broad terms about your company's presence on the Internet. Take a step back, and ask yourself these questions about your business or company:

- *Who are we as a company on the Internet?*
- *What image do we want to create for our business?*
- *Who are our customers on the Internet?*
- *What pain factors drive our customers to buy?*
- *What do we clearly NOT want to be perceived as?*

Every keyword you pick will directly correlate to the answers to these questions.

From these answers, you will create your **positioning statement,** which is not unlike a mission statement. However, a positioning statement asks more specific questions:

- *How do you want people to perceive your business on the Internet? What position do you want to occupy in their minds?*

And then it should state, in 200 words or less:

- *What value proposition are you trying to convey to your target search engine customer?*

Shift your mindset away from the Internet model for a minute and consider the positioning of eateries like McDonald's™ versus the Olive Garden™ versus Spago™ restaurant in Beverly Hills. They occupy very different positions within their marketplace and each has a clear identity and target audience.

Here is a sample positioning statement for an Internet company that sells designer purses:

> Our company provides customers with genuine, name brand, high-end, designer purses and handbags that are guaranteed and certified to be authentic. Our company can be trusted to provide the real thing.
>
> We offer competitive pricing along with the convenience of online purse shopping from the convenience of the customer's home with no need to waste time, sit in traffic, spend money on gas, or battle crowds.

"We are THE online source for designer purses, with a wide selection of top name brands and styles including Gucci™, Prada™, and Coach™ available in all colors and materials.

Our customers are fashion conscious, wealthy females of all ages who want current styles and the best of the best."

The point of your positioning statement is to ensure that you and everyone you hire—from your web designer to anyone connected with marketing your site—is clear and consistent about the message, image, and position you want to convey with your search engine marketing. It clarifies how you will present and promote your business on the Internet, and will serve as a guide to your keyword discovery process. All keywords, ads, and landing pages will consistently communicate this positioning to all your search engine customers.

Your aim in creating a positioning statement is for you to know exactly what your company provides to customers; what it does not do; what market space you occupy (position); and to whom you sell. You need to be absolutely clear about who your customers are.

If you sell high-end designer purses, then you absolutely, positively do not want to be associated with knockoffs or bargains of any kind because that's *not* who you are or the position you occupy. Unless you want to pay for every single click from anybody anywhere looking for purses—most of whom do not want what you're selling, you must *define your market, your position,* and your *value proposition* very carefully and specifically, *and figure out who your customers are and HOW they shop for your products online.*

The goal here is to:

1. Narrowly identify your audience/prospects
2. Figure out the terms by which those prospects will search for you
3. Differentiate yourself in your narrowed market space

Numbers 1 and 3 are up to you; those are about your business and your branding. Number 2 is what we're here to help with.

Step 2: The Brainstorming Session

We have been executing this exact process with clients for years, and you will be surprised what comes out of this session. Please don't skip this step, because it's essential that you break free from the keywords that you automatically associate with your business and automatically assume what people use to search for your product or service. Instead, we're going to encourage you to hear what your *customers* are telling you every day. To do so, you must bring everyone in your company together and have a brainstorming session.

Invitees

The most important thing about this session is who (or whom) you invite. If you're a large company, you need to understand that when we say invite everyone we mean *everyone*—from sales to customer service to information technology (IT). You don't want only management and executives at this meeting; crucial people such as your salesforce, your customer service reps, your service department, your front desk clerks, and your receptionists are all on the *front line* with customers every day. You want to hear from the people who talk to customers, because that's who knows their concerns best. They are aware of what they're looking for when they call or come in, what they're asking for and about, and what *words* they're using to do so. Every one of these people has valuable input, which is exactly how you start to build your keywords; to ignore them is to bypass a massive amount of intelligence about your company (see Figure 6.1).

Figure 6.1   "This is Mrs. McBride from Marketing."

Cartoonbank.com. Used with permission.

I recently had an automotive client that was getting poor results from its paid search campaign. I asked members of the company how they came up with their keywords, since the terms that they had used seemed sort of high level for an endeavor intended to drive online sales. I discovered that they had assumed that they knew how customers searched for their business; yet they had never even asked the staff who answered their phones on a daily basis what the most common questions or requests were, what people asked for or wanted to know, and how they asked. *Those* are the people who know the customers' pain factors and problems best. *They're* the ones to whom customers are talking when they're frustrated, upset, need help, or something is broken. They're the ones who hear: *Do you have . . . ? Where do I find . . . ? My . . . isn't working. I need to replace the . . . Someone just told me I need . . .* and so on.

You can certainly invite the executive team and management to the brainstorming session; it's probably best, however, to ask them to reserve any "management-specific" comments until the session is over (though they're welcome to shout out words and ideas along with everyone else). You'll get the best meeting dynamic if the staff can speak freely without any fear of repercussion from the bosses.

If you're a small company without a lot of employees, it's still important that everyone in the company is present and has equal say and equal freedom to write down or yell out whatever comes to mind. And if you're a sole proprietor, then invite your friends, colleagues, and a few good customers to lunch and do this.

The critical thing is to actually *do* the brainstorming; don't assume that you already know your keywords.

Setting Up the Session

It's a good idea to schedule the brainstorming session for after hours, or over lunch. Forward the phone calls to an answering service, or hire a temp. Get huge stacks of the biggest Sticky Notes you can find. Make ample food and caffeine available. Take an "old school" approach to the session, and set up a half-dozen easels, whiteboards, or chalkboards at the front of the room. Give each attendee a large stack of sticky notes and a pen.

Ground Rules for the Brainstorming Session

Set some ground rules for the session, one of which should be that there is no such thing as a wrong or stupid answer or thought. Every possible idea anyone can think of gets shouted out, written down on a sticky note, and stuck on a board at the front of the room or written on the whiteboards. No negative input is allowed. No groaning or rolling of eyes. The purpose of this session is broad keyword exploration. Sometimes the highest performing keywords come out of these sessions.

Before your group is contaminated by any suggestions on what you want from the session, ask them this one question: **"How would you search for our product or service on the web?"** Since each person will have a different perspective on this, don't ruin it by asking leading or probing questions. In fact, don't do anything else until every person has finished his or her own sticky note writing.

Whiteboards

Once you've collected everyone's sticky notes, write these words in large type at the top of the whiteboards:

- Sticky Note Keywords
- Pain Factors—Problems Customers Have
  — For example, "Broken TV," "Sick Cat"
- Company Offerings
  — For example, "TV Repair," "Vet Services"
- Obvious, General Terms
  — For example, "Television," "Vaccinations")
- Common Customer Terms
- Location, Geographic Terms
  — For example, "Charleston TV," "Charleston Vet")
- Products (generic descriptions)
- Branded, Industry Terms
  — For example, "HD TV Repair," "FrontLine flea medication")

- Things We Don't Do: Negative Keywords
  — For example, "Cable Box Repair," "Large Animal Vet")
- Seasonality
  — For example, "Start of Football Season," "Spring Pet Vacci-
    nations")

Give everyone an equal role in collaboratively answering the following questions from the customer's point of view by stepping into their shoes. Have them simply shout out the answers.

Pain Factor Questions
- What are the pain factors that drive people to our product or services? What are our customers' *problems*? What are they needing/wanting/looking for/hoping for?
- If I were a person with "x" problem, need, or wish, why would I want to find our company in my Internet search?

Common Terms: Your Own and Customers
- What would I be looking for? What would I call it? How might I phrase it? How do I think about it?
- What words or phrases do people use when they call our company inquiring about our product or service, or when they have questions or problems?
- What words or phrases do they use when talking to others about our product or service? (Although "Fast Food" might be the broad category that McDonald's™ falls into, people don't usually say to each other "let's go get a fast food lunch.")

Products
- Run through every product that you sell in its generic description and every permutation and combination in terms of make,

model, size, and color (unless you have a catalog or database that you can simply upload).

Seasonality
- What are the company's seasons; how do our terms and products change by season?

Geography
- Where and to whom do we sell?

General Probing Questions
- What is the purpose of marketing our business on the Internet, and who are we hoping to drive to our site?
- What are the features and benefits of what we offer?
- How do we NOT want to be found on the Internet?

Everyone participates during this session, and your job as the facilitator is to keep the session high energy, fun, and open to any and all ideas and input.

What Do All These Questions Have to Do with Keywords?

Your keyword list will come out of this process. At the end of the session, your job will be to compile all the words that everyone contributed into a single document. This is the beginning of your NEW keyword list. Excel is an excellent tool for organizing your keywords because the spreadsheet format helps you manipulate your lists in an easy way and will make the process of uploading your final list easier. Although it's not necessary, it will also help you to automate the process.

A good goal is to amass from 50 to 100 keywords from your brainstorming session. While this may seem like a lot, the more robust and complete you can make your list in this phase, the easier job you will have later, and the better your campaign will perform.

A Simple Example of How This Process Works

Imagine that you work for or manage a plumbing company. The keywords that may initially come to mind during your brainstorming session are: *plumbing, plumbers, plumbing services, plumbing repairs.* Maybe your city is attached; so you might come up with *plumbing repairs Austin,* or *Austin plumber.* And don't forget misspellings such as *plummer* and *plumer.* After your brainstorming session—where everyone's hopped up on caffeine and shouting out whatever comes into their heads—you may end up with the terms that customers actually use when they need a plumber; and then your keyword list might look more like this: *stopped-up toilet, overflowing toilet, leaking toilet, clogged sink, hair-clogged drain, leaking sink, leaking pipes, broken pipes, broken faucet, backed-up sewer, tree roots in sewer.*

Another Example

Let's return to the designer purse example. You might think that it would be easy to just skip the brainstorming session, because you know what you do. You sell designer purses. What more do you need to know?

However, if your market space is designer purses, your customers will expect you to be the authority in the designer handbag space. And the way you show them that you *are* the authority and that you deserve their business, is to speak *their* language by using *their* search terms as the keywords in your PPC ad campaigns. On an elementary level, this means perhaps calling your products *purses*; or perhaps *handbags* or *pocketbooks*; or just *designer bags*. All those terms should be on your keyword list. Maybe your customers use the term *designer* or *couture* or maybe they think in terms of *name-brand* or *high-end* purses. Have those words on the list as well.

At a more sophisticated and detailed level—say, if your customer is looking for the *Coach™ Hamptons Leather Carryall in Berry*—they'll be impressed if those words show up on the results page; and they'll be likely to click on your ad. And if a common question is whether the Hamptons Carryall comes in only brass or also in brushed nickel hardware, show your customers that you're such an authority in this market space that you can anticipate that question and answer it for them using their own search terms, so that your result says *available in brass only*.

Your keywords will illustrate your company's authority and education in your market space. If you speak to them at every stage of their search—from the general *designer handbags*, to *Coach™ Leather Carryall*, to *Leather Carryall Berry Brass Hardware*—your company wins their business by establishing trust and credibility every time they see your ad.

The point of the brainstorming exercise is to build your keyword list with your customers' desires, wishes, wants, hopes, problems, or needs in mind and by using the words, terms, and language they use to search for the solution to their quest.

A Few More Notes on Your Keyword Ideas

You must take care to remember the following points when compiling your keyword list:

- *Company name and web address:* Always include the company name and your web domain name or names in your keyword list, because that's certainly one of the ways that people will search for you. (Note: Even though you might think that people know the difference between the address bar and the search box, you'd be mistaken. Trust me, lots of people type URLs, or web addresses, into the search box. So make sure your domain name, in every permutation, is included in your keywords: mydomainname.com, www.mydomainname.com, http://mydomainname.com. That way, anyone looking for you will find you no matter what they type in or where they type it.)

- *Frequent errors:* Include common mistakes as well as common misspellings of your keywords and your company name. Your front line—down to your receptionist and your mail person—can tell you all the ways people mangle your company name, brand name, building name, and your other search terms. For example, *Banana Republic* can be found under its correct spelling and also under *Bananna Republic* and *Bannana Republic,* because the company KNOWS that people will search for them with those spellings. Gucci™ can be found under its common misspellings, as can Ferrari™. *Hilton Head, South Carolina,* can also be found under *Hilton Head, North Carolina,* because the folks at the Hilton Head hotels and resorts know that most people don't know *which* Carolina they're in. And while you can find me under *Lutze* for either my company name or my personal name, you should be able to find me under *Lutz* also!

- *Your product list or catalog:* If you have already gone to the effort of building out a catalog of all your products with pricing, product numbers, colors, brand names, manufactures, and any other relevant information, then all these items should be added to your core keyword list under a category of "Product Names."

- *Seasonality:* Seasonality is an important part of building out your keyword list and of arranging your keywords by group and theme later on. In fact, it is so important that Chapter 9—Seasonality—is devoted to it. Thinking in terms of "seasons" will help you expand your keyword list in many ways—since people cook different food, wear different clothes, buy different products, seek different services, and consider major purchases in various seasonal patterns. It may also start to plant some seeds for ad group and ad campaigns; in fact, many businesses have "hidden seasons"—even those that think they don't.

The subject of seasonality is not just relevant for businesses that know they have seasons (though it will help them make sure they include all their seasonal terms, or will remind, say a greenhouse, to include poinsettias and wreaths in their keywords). So even if you're sure your business doesn't have a seasonal aspect, please read Chapter 9, and your opinion may change.

Once you've used your positioning statement and brainstorming session to compile a long list of keywords covering every category and word you can think of, you will move on to using a more "databased" method for expanding your keyword list even further.

Step 3: Using a Keyword Research Tool

Note: Using a keyword research tool should only be done *after* you've completed the brainstorming session.

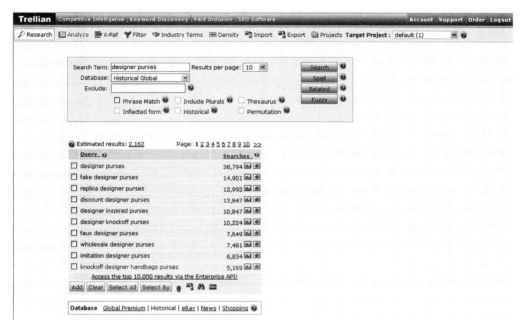

Figure 6.2   **Keyword Research Tool**

Used with permission from Keyword Discovery.

What Is a Keyword Research Tool?

A keyword research tool is a data aggregator of customer keyword search activity on the Internet (see Figure 6.2). It can provide you with all the possible related terms and term combinations for your broad, generic search terms (also called the **root term** or **core term;** e.g., *televisions, purses, auto parts, computers, plumbing*). Not only does it give you all the related terms and combinations; it also shows you misspellings, similar keywords, and other keyword data.

These tools also offer data for the searches performed under each term (called **search volume**). This will help you prioritize and pick your terms for the greatest performance over a period of time.

The research details not only the keywords that are being *actively* searched in your market space, it also provides historical searches and predicted clicks over a given time frame—such as keyword searches over the period of a month or a year. You enter each keyword, and this tool shows you the search volume for your core term—and all its related terms.

This data will help you determine your top volume terms and which keywords you want to use for your beginning campaigns (if you can't afford to run them all). This tool will allow you to evaluate your keywords in terms of cost, budget, and your informational, shopping and purchasing keywords from a search volume standpoint.

Each of the search engines provides a basic keyword research tool. However, we suggest that you use a more sophisticated version. Many advertisers are not aware that other versions exist, so making this upgrade will help put you and keep you ahead of the competition.

There are several keyword research tools on the market, and they all have their strengths and unique attributes. They also each display their results differently. Some have great graphics and are especially easy to read. Most tools easily export into an Excel spreadsheet or similar download for manipulation and organization. Some offer intermediate and advanced information. Costs vary from a one-time fee to a monthly fee for subscribing to their web site, and some are free as part of your PPC campaign.

The tools have the following in common:
- They can show you the keywords in your industry, including common misspellings, seasonal search trends, and keyword density analysis (ideal repetition of the keyword in your web content).

- They can help you find all keyword combinations that bear any relation to your business, service, or product—many of which you may never have considered.
- They will provide a database of terms that people search. You enter certain keywords and the tools can tell you how often people search for them, and also tell you how many competing sites use those keywords.

Your keyword research tool is going to be one of your most important resources; so look at what the different providers offer and choose the one that gives you the best information for your particular business. Most of these tools provide a 24-hour or 30-day free evaluation period for you to test-drive the tools.

Here are a few keyword research tools for you to check out:

Trellian Keyword Discovery
http://www.KeywordDiscovery.com
- Subscription-based tool
- Free Trial Version
- Compiles search statistics from over 200 search engines world-wide
- 36 billion searches tracked over 12 months

Wordtracker
http://www.WordTracker.com
- Subscription-based tool
- Helps web site owners and search engine marketers identify keywords and phrases that are relevant to their business or their client's business and most likely to be used as queries by search engine visitors

- Can also determine how many competing sites are using those keywords and can identify the phrases that have the greatest traffic potential

Google Keyword Tool

https://adwords.google.com/select/KeywordToolExternal

- This is a free tool that you can access through your Google AdWords account or use this link to access it externally.

MSN adCenter Excel Add-In Tool

http://advertising.microsoft.com/search-advertising/adcenter_addin

- This is Microsoft's real-time search tool for MSN.net and MSN-Live account holders. The adCenter Add-in Beta is a keyword research and optimization tool based in Excel that includes the Ad Intelligence model, which enables you to:
  — Easily and quickly build out or expand keyword lists.
  — Effectively plan keyword strategy based relevance, cost history, volume, demographics, geography, and more.
  — Forecast monthly and daily keyword impressions and future trends.

Also, be sure to check www.FindabilityFormula.com from time to time, because we'll post new tools there as they become available.

When reviewing the keyword searches in your industry, I recommend that you look at a data set that spans at least a full year, because keywords trend by season (see Figure 6.3). If you only look at a week or a month, you could be getting skewed and misleading information Chapter 9—Seasonality.

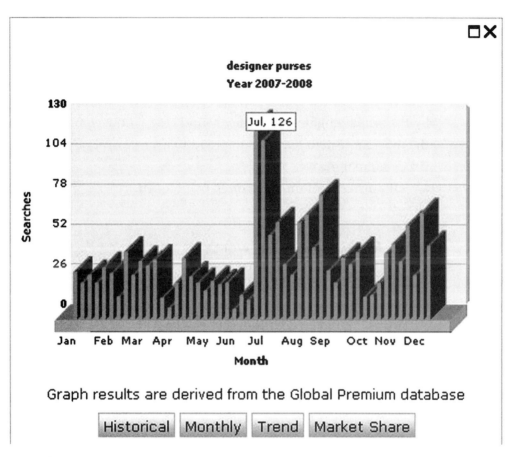

Figure 6.3   **Keyword Trend by Season**

Source: Global Premium database. Keyword Discovery. Used with permission.

Summary

Use a keyword research tool when choosing the keywords for your paid search campaign. Often the keywords you BELIEVE are best are very different from the ones that the tools provide. (This might be an indication that you're not plugged into HOW your customers search for your services.)

Step 4: Negative Keywords

Now that you have completed your keyword research and explored every avenue and term for how you do want to be found on the Internet, it's time to figure out how you DO NOT want to be found by the search engines. This may sound crazy; however, it's one of the most important steps on the road to a successful pay per click (PPC) campaign.

It's also one of the most often overlooked.

What Are Negative Keywords?

Negative or Excluded keywords are the list of search terms under which you do NOT want to show up in search results. Google AdWords, Yahoo! Search Marketing, and MSN adCenter all offer you the option of selecting Negative or Excluded Keywords to add to your account.

This option is important because *search engines make matching decisions on your behalf,* and if you don't have a list of negative keywords in your PPC accounts, you could end up paying for wasted clicks. By missing the chance to determine how you do NOT want to be found, you are letting Google, Yahoo! or MSN match your ad to what *they* think is relevant, rather than to what you *know* is relevant. This can hurt your branding, identity, and market position, not to mention the MONEY THAT YOU ARE WASTING by paying for a click for someone looking for something you don't sell or offer.

Let's say that you're in the business of selling fine timepieces, such as Rolex™, Breitling™, and Patek Philippe™, and that each one of those brand names is in your keyword campaign. If you offer authentic, certified watches, you will want to exclude certain words from your account so that you do NOT show up in any searches that include the word knockoffs, discount, imitation, or fake.

If someone types "fake Rolex" into the search bar, and fake is not one of your negative keywords, then you will show up in that search—which is a bad result for you and the searcher.

If you create a list of negative keywords and include them in your ad campaign, then you will not show up on any search results page in response to a search for fake or knockoffs or imitations. By using negative keywords, you exclude yourself from Rolex searches that aren't looking for the real thing.

It's important to do this for the following reasons:

- Why pay for a wasted click? People looking for fake Rolexes are not your customers and they're not going to buy from you.
- You do not want to be associated with cheap imitations in any way; that is not your positioning, and you shouldn't be showing up in those results.

So, if you sell cars, and not car parts and you don't do car rental, exclude the terms *parts* and *rental.* If you sell silk flowers, let the search engines know not to match you with any search for fresh flowers by putting *fresh* or *live* in your negative keywords. If you vaccinate pets, and not people, put *people, human,* and *travel* in your list of negative keywords, so that someone needing shots for a trip to Bangladesh doesn't click on your ad. While you're at it, add *child* and *school* to your negative keywords. If you sell real guns and don't exclude *toy* from your search terms, then you're going to get some customers looking for toy guns. Excluding the term *toy* will help you avoid wasted clicks and will help your user avoid a bad search experience.

Sometimes, there's no way to circumvent certain mismatches. There are terms that have multiple meanings that the search engines can't differentiate between or among. The keyword *Internet speaker* can mean a presenter or speakers for your computer. I know which one I want to pay for and which one is non-relevant; however, the search engine does not, and there's really no way to correct that. Since I don't want to exclude the term, I just live with some non-relevant clicks.

Help Finding Your Negative Keywords

To aid in building out your negative keyword list, Google AdWords provides a negative keyword suggestion tool inside their Keyword Tool. This tool will tell you all the intelligent associations being made on your campaign keywords. These keywords will change seasonally, so keep a close eye on them and keep adding new negatives each month. Make sure to set your calendar or Outlook settings to remind you to check your negative suggestions in Google's Keyword Tool (see Figure 6.4).

A Real-Life Negative Keyword Illustration

A few weeks ago, my cat became quite ill. I went to my computer and typed *Emergency Vet Clinic Parker Colorado* into the search box. All the search results that came back—including the *paid ads*—were for *human* emergency room facilities. While I did get a bunch of emergency clinic listings, every single one of them should NOT have showed up as a search result for me. They were useless to me and equally useless to every organization that appeared on that page.

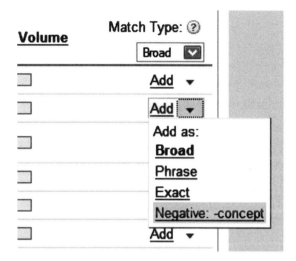

Figure 6.4   **Negative Keywords**

Google screenshots © Google Inc. Used with permission.

Whoever was in charge of the search engine marketing for those services did not bother to identify how they did NOT want to be found. They obviously put together a generic list of keywords, set the account on "broad match"—and off they went. Not every emergency search is a good candidate for their services; however, they didn't bother to exclude those that aren't. "Animal" or "Veterinary" would have been excellent words for them to exclude. I can think of a few other exclusions such as "plumbing emergency" or "hair emergency" as well.

It takes thought and effort, and identifying your negative keywords is a critical part of building a successful PPC campaign. The third-party keyword research tools that we talked about in this chapter will also help you identify negative keywords for your ad campaigns. However, don't confuse mistakes, errors, or misspellings with negative keywords. They are not the same thing. You

DO want to be found under common mistakes and misspellings, whereas you do NOT want to be found under your negative keywords.

You do NOT want to add North Carolina to your list of negative keywords if you're a hotel in Hilton Head, South Carolina. You want to include this common error in your keywords—this is truly knowing your customers inside and out and catering to them even if they make a mistake.

By utilizing the negative keyword function to the fullest, you will separate yourself from your competitors and make the most of every click you pay for. Advertisers who take advantage of this tactic get better, more qualified visibility for their ads and ultimately get better conversions for their investment dollar.

Take-Aways

- Keywords will make or break your search marketing campaigns.
- Don't just pick a bunch of obvious industry keywords and rush to get your campaigns up and running.
- Taking time up front to uncover the right keywords for your business will pay off in the end.
- Finding the right (converting) keywords is a four-step process. The goal of all four steps is to narrowly identify your prospects or customers and the terms they use to find your product or service.
- Build a negative keyword list that will help you avoid paying for clicks you don't want.

Tools You Use in This Chapter
- Keyword Discovery, KeywordDiscovery.com
- Wordtracker, Wordtracker.com
- Google Keyword Tool, https://adwords.google.com/select/KeywordToolExternal
- MSN Excel Add-In Tool, http://advertising.microsoft.com/search-advertising/adcenter_addin

CHAPTER 7

Grouping and Themeing to Complete the Keyword List

You now have a fairly comprehensive list of keywords thanks to your positioning statement, your brainstorming, keyword research tools, and your negative keywords. We call this list your "core terms" and whether it is a pile of yellow sticky notes, some sheets of legal paper, the whiteboards of your conference room, or an Excel spreadsheet, you're now going to arrange it into a format that will:

- Help you see any gaps in your terms
- Help with writing your ads
- Make setting up your campaigns as easy as possible

Your next step is to organize your core terms into logical groups by theme. You will then flesh out the list of keywords by adding modifiers to the core terms to build a more comprehensive and detailed list. During this process, the keyword list might expand by a factor of 10 or even more. If your initial core list was say 50 words, you might finally end up with a keyword list of 500 or even 5,000. The more keywords that you produce, the more broad your coverage. There's a practical limit in terms of time, of course; and keep pushing to come up with the best possible and most complete list of keywords.

Grouping is a method of building out your final keyword list. It will also provide a basic foundation and sense of organization as you move into the ad-writing phase of your campaign. The better organized the list is, the easier your job will be when you are composing your targeted ads and the more organized your site will be, making it easier for search engines to understand and know what it is about. It will help you see what you should provide searchers from the first step in their search until the end of their path. This translates into your ultimate goal, CONVERSIONS.

Organizing and Refining Your Keywords

The concept of organizing your keywords is simple, and it is best illustrated by example. Let's start with a sample keyword build for a company we'll call ABC Computer Company. We're going to follow ABC through all the steps of keyword discovery and bring them to the process of grouping and themeing.

ABC Computer Company

Like many firms, ABC Computer Company started with a basic, simple, and generic keyword list; ran a pay per click (PPC) campaign with this list; spent some money; and received very few results. They then shut their campaign off, because they felt that PPC ads didn't work for them. Here is the keyword list they used:

Keywords from Old Campaign
- Computer
- PC
- Gaming Computer
- Gaming PC

No wonder they didn't get results!

So we walked ABC Computer Company through the keyword process.

First we had them create a *positioning statement* that read:

Positioning Statement of ABC Computer Company

We specialize in high-end gaming and high-performance computers for adults. Our demographic is mostly male with an average annual income of over $100K. Our designs are modern and progressive for serious enthusiasts who want a fun and hip look for their computer. They want to play the newest games and have fast processing speeds and functionality. Our average computer build-outs start at $3,000 per unit and up. We sell ONLY desktops that are customized to exact specification orders. We offer free shipping and a 30-day, money-back guarantee.

Notice that ABC has answered all the pertinent questions in their position statement: who they are; what product/service they make or offer; who they sell to; their average prices; and even the extras that make them different from their competitors.

Next, we had ABC *brainstorm* a comprehensive list of keywords. After discussing several ideas with the staff, ABC Computer Company came up with a new list of words generated mostly by their employees, who are primarily gaming coders and techies. The technical support and phone support staff came to the table with niche-based terms that were important to them when buying computers for themselves and that were not apparent to the executive or marketing teams. Although one might assume that the management and marketing teams would already be aware of these terms, different departments within an organization often don't communicate with each other. In addition, they collected keywords from their web site analytics and added those to the mix.

In fact, the staff had a unique connection with the customers and the exact features and brands they were looking for in their new computers as well as the terms that would be most important to potential customers (e.g., *Melee Monster Masher 6000* is the company's bestselling computer).

Here is an abbreviated version of their new and improved keyword list:

Brainstorming Keywords
- Quad Core Gaming Computer
- Nvidia Graphics Computer
- Liquid Cooled Computer
- ATI Radeon Gaming Computer
- Overclocking Gaming Computer
- Melee Monster Masher 6000

Note: This example is abbreviated for the purpose of the book. Fully built-out examples and spreadsheets can be found online at www .FindabilityFormula. com.

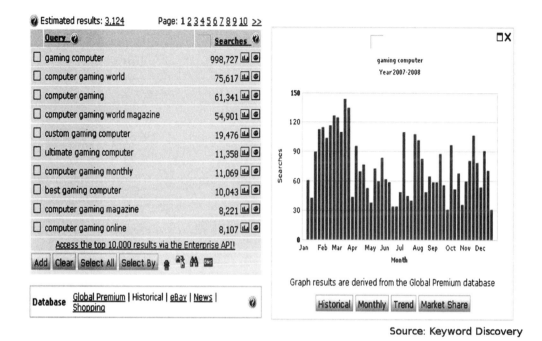

Source: Keyword Discovery

Figure 7.1   **Keyword Discovery Estimated Results**

Screen shots taken from KeywordDiscovery.com, historical global database. Used with permission.

We then had ABC use a ***keyword discovery tool*** to find additional keyword data—in this case, KeywordDiscovery.com. They began with the keywords from their original campaign and the list from their brainstorming session, and looked at historical keyword data that showed them search volumes for their terms by month and a seasonal trending report. They also examined additional keyword suggestions and related terms that had high search volumes and should be added to their list or account. Figure 7.1 shows what that looked like.

As a result of these three steps, ABC came up with a new keyword spreadsheet with the three groups of data they gathered:

Keywords from Old Campaign	Brainstorming Terms	Keyword Tool Terms
Computer	Quad Core Gaming Computer	Computer gaming world
PC	Nvidia Graphics Computer	Computer gaming
Gaming Computer	Liquid Cooled Computer	Computer gaming world magazine
Gaming PC	ATI Radeon Gaming Computer	Custom gaming computer
Gaming Desktop	Overclocking Gaming Computer	Ultimate gaming computer

Note: This example is abbreviated for the purpose of the book. Fully built-out examples and spreadsheets can be found at www.FindabilityFormula.com.

Once these steps have been completed in your own company, it is time for you to undertake Keyword Themeing and Grouping.

Keyword Themeing and Grouping

Your job now is to look for common themes and trends in your list and put them in buckets, groups by similar topics or themes. For the same computer example, we now have the following grouping of terms that apply to gaming computers.

ABC Company might have one bucket for the **Generic—Old Keywords,** a bucket for **Niche Gaming** keywords, and a bucket for **High Volume Gaming** keywords. The buckets might look like this:

Keywords	Bucket/Theme
Computer	Generic—Old Keywords
PC	Generic—Old Keywords
Gaming Computer	Generic—Old Keywords
Gaming PC	Generic—Old Keywords
Quad Core Gaming Computer	Niche Gaming
Nvidia Graphics Computer	Niche Gaming
Liquid Cooled Computer	Niche Gaming
ATI Radeon Gaming Computer	Niche Gaming
Computer gaming world	High Volume Gaming
Computer gaming	High Volume Gaming
Computer gaming world magazine	High Volume Gaming
Custom gaming computer	High Volume Gaming
Ultimate gaming computer	High Volume Gaming

Now they will need to build out a complete list of all keywords grouped by bucket, or theme. This list should have buckets in as much detail as possible, including brands, screen sizes, special features, price points—any information that is relevant for grouping products.

You will know best which modifiers—brands, sizes, seasons, makes, models, features, colors, and service descriptions—apply to your own business. If your product or service has a geographic component, be sure to create the appropriate buckets and add your geographic modifiers (see Chapter 8), such as *New England, Vermont, Burlington, Vermont, Stratton Mountain, Vermont*—all of which would all be appropriate keywords and terms for a person searching for a gaming computer in Vermont.

Grouping Keywords by Customer Experience

We group and theme keywords to create the optimal *customer* experience. When customers are looking for a new gaming computer and they type in the keywords *liquid cooled gaming computer* as their search term, they expect to get a *liquid cooled* computer search result page. If they click on a *liquid cooled* ad, they expect to be delivered to a relevant *liquid cool* information page. The more specific the keyword they search under, the more specific the page you need to take them to in response. So if all your related terms are grouped together, you can create one ad, one landing page, and one seamless, relevant experience for the user.

Why Are We Having You Go to All This Trouble?

In the search marketing world, bucketing or themeing is the way you create a solid path to a high-quality experience for anyone searching under your keywords. By paying attention to all the elements of searchers' requests for information along their "path to purchase"—from their first keyword search, to their longer strings, to the moment that they're ready to buy, and where you land them on your site at each stage—you are carefully crafting each step to respond to your customers' **need.**

This is the first step in delivering **relevant results,** which is the first step to a quality **path to purchase** experience for your customers and prospective customers. Grouping or categorizing these keywords now will ensure the most custom relevant user experience possible. *Users* are pleased because they have been given relevant results every step of the way. *You* are rewarded for providing a good search experience to your customers because they are purchasing your product or service. And the *search engine*s actually assign ratings based on your customers' experience. Those ratings translate into good placement on a results page and lower costs for your clicks.

In other words—everyone wins.

Organization

Bucketing also keep you organized and ensures that you leave nothing out of your keyword lists. It allows you to see your own themes and to check if anything is missing. What kinds of products did you neglect to mention? What styles, colors, make, or model numbers did you leave out? What features that people often search by did you forget to include?

When we're talking about keywords at this level of detail and with this number of keywords (remember: we're going for 500 or more), organizing the search terms by group or theme is a must. Not only for now, but when you start to write your ads, the words need to be in buckets (unless you want to write 500 separate ads.)

Grouping According to the Buying Cycle

In addition to grouping by theme, it's also a smart strategy to **group your keywords according to your customer's *buying cycle*.** This will affect the way you bucket your keywords when your particular customer gets closer to buying. Both strategies are equally valid, and one is sometimes more effective than the other under certain conditions. Generally, the *combination of both—by theme and by buying cycle*—produces the best results. Test both. Find out what works best for your business.

With the *buying cycle keyword approach,* we ask this question: *Which keywords need to be most available to customers at what point in their decision/buying cycle?* It's not just about search volume; it's about giving customers the right keyword at the right time in their decision-making process.

As an advertiser, you must have a basic understanding of your particular market, and your customers' usual buying cycle. Is your product or service simple or complex? Is the decision-making process usually short or long? What is the normal sales process for your specific product or service?

Keyword Combinations and Variables

Creating extensive keyword lists can produce exponential keyword combinations. If you multiply the brand, product, model, color, size, and feature combinations by each other in all possible combinations, you get into the many thousands. We recommend including all the combinations in your paid search account and you only pay for what actually performs (what people click on).

There *is* a point of diminishing returns where you are wasting your efforts for search terms that will never receive any search volume. You need to edit your list intelligently and evaluate any keywords that have more than five or six elements. It's important to know when to stop the creation process and begin to test for results.

In addition to brands, features, sizes, colors, and other product attributes, *location* may be an important element of keyword grouping. Cities, counties, states, countries, and neighborhoods are relevant search terms for some types of business and are less relevant for others. We fully explore this concept in Chapter 8—Location, Location, Location.

Take-Aways

- Enter all the keyword terms from your keyword discovery process into a spreadsheet.
- Organize and group them by theme, fill in any missing terms, categories, combinations, and variables.
- Bucket your keywords by buying cycle, customer experience, category, location, campaign, or season . . . whatever makes sense for your business.

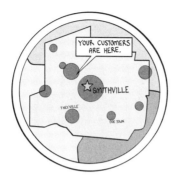

CHAPTER 8

Location, Location, Location

If you have a physical location in addition to your online presence, location is always important, especially for last-minute shoppers who want to find what they're looking for online, and who may want to shop locally to make a purchase. For those with a short buying window (e.g., their mother-in-law's birthday is tomorrow, and they need something *now)*, a city, neighborhood, or zip code can be an important search criterion. Online purchasers will often also check a "ship from" location and choose the one closest to them for shorter delivery times.

Once you've built your keyword list, you need to think about how it's going to be geographically structured inside your pay per click (PPC) accounts. Do you want or need to limit your campaigns by geography? If so, you can geographically target your campaigns in one of two ways:

1. Geotargeting
2. Adding geographic modifiers

Geotargeting

Geotargeting enables you to limit the *visibility* of your ad to certain geographic locations. With this approach, you control who will actually *see* the ad. The big three search engines allow you to geotarget any of your campaigns, which means your ad will appear only within certain geographic areas that you choose.

You have to give careful thought when deciding what works for your particular business and target market. And it's also possible that you don't need either. If your market is the whole country, or the whole world, then geography is not a factor for you. And if you're a flooring installer or a landscaping service in Sarasota, Florida, then it might make sense to geotarget or use geographic modifiers.

Within any ad campaign, you can specify that if a customer types in *landscape services* or *flooring installer,* you only want your company to show up for searches being conducted from the Sarasota, Florida, metro area. And if you sell laptop computers—and your market is the whole world—you wouldn't want or need to geotarget.

Geographic Modifiers

Geographic modifiers do NOT limit who SEES your ad; instead, they indicate geographic areas within the keyword string, so you can capture the searchers and reach a more targeted audience. Sometimes you will want to use one of these techniques without using the other one; it depends on what you sell, to whom, and what areas you want to sell to.

Geotargeting versus Geographic Modifiers

Figuring out when to geotarget and when to modify keywords with geographic indicators without limiting who sees the ad can be tricky. Let's say that you're in Sacramento, California, and you sell leather couches. You might say to yourself, *I'm going to run leather couches as one of my keywords, and I only want my ad displayed to Sacramento metro searchers, because that's where there are people who are likely to be my customers.* So you'd run a geotargeted campaign that will be seen only by people in your area. And you wouldn't even need to put "Sacramento" into every keyword string, because you are already geotargeting the ad for Sacramento area searches through your campaign settings. An exception to this is that search engines do not have geotargeting down as an exact science and you might miss out on some impressions.

What if a 30-something couple is moving from Memphis to Sacramento and wants to know where to buy their new couch when they get there? If you've geotargeted Sacramento, they won't see your ad because they're not in Sacramento when they're searching. And what if your business is a moving company and you move people from anywhere in the county to Sacramento? Would you want to geotarget Sacramento?

In both these cases, you would want to run a *nationwide* (not geotargeted) campaign and include geographic modifiers, such as the keyword phrase *leather couches **Sacramento,** moving company **Sacramento*** or *moving company **California.*** That way, anyone searching from anywhere in the country that needs to relocate to or from Sacramento or wants to buy furniture in Sacramento will see you in their search results.

Another Example

Let's look at another example. If you run a whitewater rafting company in Colorado, you would *not* want to geotarget for Colorado, because your market is the whole country, or even the world. Geotargeting for Colorado wouldn't allow anyone else in the country to see the ad. You would, however, want to use geographic modifiers in your keyword string such as *Whitewater rafting Colorado* or *Colorado Whitewater rafting.* This way, anyone searching for these services for Colorado will come across your company.

Recommendation

Some advertisers are not sure whether geotargeting or geographic modifiers make sense for their business. If you don't know whether and how this is applicable to your company, my recommendation is to start your PPC campaigns by choosing the U.S. delivery option so that your ad can be seen by anyone in the United States, and then add a state geographic modifier, such as Colorado or California. Then create a geotargeted campaign that is only shown to people in your state. Run both campaigns, and see what produces the best results.

Careful thought, experimentation and examination of your results will guide you to whether and how location plays a part in your ad campaigns.

Example: A U.S. Delivery Campaign with Geographic Modifiers

If you're going to run a campaign with geographic modifiers, you'll do yourself a favor if you come up with all the possible permutations that you can think of. Here's an example of what we mean using the preceding rafting scenario. Setting your ad on U.S. Delivery will display it to anyone, anywhere in the United States who types in any of these terms:

- River Rafting Colorado
- River rafting Colorado
- River rafting Colo
- River rafting CO
- River rafting Denver Colorado
- River rafting Denver Colo
- River rafting Denver CO
- River rafting Denver area
- River rafting near Denver
- River rafting near Denver CO
- River rafting Vail Colorado
- River rafting Aspen Colorado
- River rafting Estes Park Colorado
- *You get the picture . . . .*

Now here's an example of search terms you might use for ads that will only show up to people searching from the area you targeted (e.g., Colorado only):

- River rafting
- Whitewater rafting
- Whitewater river rafting
- Half-day river rafting trips
- Full-day river rafting trips
- Family rafting trips
- Beginner rafting trips
- Beginner float trips
- Intermediate river rafting
- Expert whitewater rafting

You don't need to modify the keywords with the term *Colorado* because only people in Colorado are seeing your ad.

This process might seem confusing at first; however, as you start working with it and experimenting, the concept becomes clear. More important, your ad campaign results will guide you to what works best for your particular business.

Take-Aways

- Geographic targeting has appropriate uses, advantages, and disadvantages that must be carefully considered for any campaign.
- Geotargeting means your campaigns will be visible only in certain geographic areas.
- Geographic keyword modifiers allow you to run your campaign statewide, nationwide, or worldwide while geographic references narrow your target.

CHAPTER 9

Seasonality

Seasonality is an important component in pay per click (PPC) campaigns, and comes into play in two significant ways:

1. It is an important factor in building out your keyword list.
2. It may influence when you decide to run your ad campaigns.

Yes Virginia, There Is a Santa Claus

You might not think that seasonality applies to your business; however, I challenge you to reconsider that belief. I also suggest that you go to your front line to check if they think it does.

Obviously, certain goods and services like snow removal, air conditioning repair, gardening, Christmas trees, and Valentine's Day candy trend by season, as does retail in general. But if you look deep enough, you are likely to discover that your business does as well. One of the things I tell my clients is: *Even if you don't think your business is seasonal, in the world of the Internet and keyword searches, it almost certainly is.*

Understanding the potential seasonal aspect of your business is an important part of conducting a successful paid search campaign. And this applies whether your business is product or service based.

Hidden and Subtle Seasonality

Here's an example of seasonality that might make you think differently about keywords based on time of year. Over the course of teaching Yahoo! Search Marketing Advertiser Workshops, I used the same keyword to show variations in results month after month. It is a perfect illustration of seasonality that, at first pass, you might not think even existed.

If you look at the term *cooking* during the last quarter of the calendar year (October, November, and December), you find the majority of searches are for *cooking roasts, cooking turkey,* and *cooking standing rib roast.* Come the first quarter of the year (January, February, and March), the searches suddenly shift to *low fat cooking, Atkins cooking,* and the like. Cooking is a seasonal industry and a seasonally modified keyword. If I am a cooking supply company then I care about roasting pans in fall for Thanksgiving and Christmas, and dessert molds or cupcake tins for spring celebrations, and low fat or low calorie cooking at the beginning of the year.

Many businesses have more subtle seasons. Are there certain times of the year that businesses plan their conventions, budget for large equipment purchases, or plan for the following year's training programs? The time during which a particular industry's major convention is held each year is their season. And it might make sense to market to that convention by mentioning it in your keywords and your ad text, or even going so far as to say: *Come visit us in Booth 5555, Come meet our president,* or *Live demo August 15, Register Now.* Building a campaign around that big conference might be your season.

Okay—you get the picture. You know the pulse of your business; it's now your job to flesh out the seasonal keywords from within your organization. Seasonality may factor in more often than you think.

Reverse Seasonality

Here's an example of *reverse* seasonality: I have a client who specializes in complicated tax issues. He is very careful NOT to run his PPC campaigns during March and April for the tax preparation season. He does not do regular tax returns and does not want to pay for clicks or answer inquiries about tax preparation. In fact, it's immediately AFTER April 15—when people realize they have a big problem because they didn't file on time—that he wants leads; so that's when he runs his *tax problems* keyword campaigns full throttle.

Campaign Timing

The seasonality of your business is worth thinking about—even if it's not obvious—because putting your keywords into buckets by season and running your paid search ads by season can make a big difference in a campaign's performance. People seem to forget this and simply run the same ad campaigns all year long. Wouldn't it make better sense for a gift basket company or flower store to run specific targeted campaigns at their principal holiday times? For a landscaper to target spring; accountants, tax season; air conditioning companies, the beginning of summer?

Seasonally targeted campaigns can help businesses take advantage of major and predictable opportunities in their business year. Figure 9.1 shows a chart that might help you plan when to load and launch your accounts to take full advantage of seasonal timing.

The *Marketing Experiment Journal* published this great list of the top nine retail holidays according to the National Retail Federation (http://www.nrf.com):

1. Winter Holidays
2. Back to school
3. Valentine's Day
4. Mother's Day
5. Easter
6. Father's Day
7. Super Bowl (not really a season or holiday, but it generated over $9 billion this year)
8. Halloween
9. St. Patrick's Day

If your business doesn't trend along these lines, consider creating your own seasonal campaign calendar; and certainly consider seasons in your keyword build-out and the timing of your ad campaigns.

Search Marketing Seasonal Retail Calendar

Initiative	Jan	Feb	Mar	Apr	May	Jun	Jul	Aug	Sept	Oct	Nov	Dec
Valentine's Day		14-Feb										
Launch	5-Jan											
Graduation/Prom			Mar - June									
Launch			1-Mar									
Mother's Day					8-May							
Launch			22-Mar									
Father's Day						19-Jun						
Launch					10-May							
Back to School								July 1 - Sept 30				
Launch						15-Jun						
Halloween										31-Oct		
Launch								15-Aug				
Holiday Season											Nov - Dec	
Launch								30-Aug				

Figure 9.1 **Campaign Timing**

Yahoo! Search Marketing. Used with permission.

Take-Aways

- Seasonality is an important factor in building out your keyword list and in deciding when to run your keyword campaigns.
- Even if you don't think your business has a seasonal component, it probably does. It may require some creative thinking to figure it out.

Tools You Use in This Chapter
- National Retail Federation, http://www.nrf.com

CHAPTER 10

Writing Your Ad Text

Now that you've completed the meticulous process of keyword building and organization, you have to think about the ad that your searchers will see when they've typed in their keyword and hit "search."

What Is an "Ad"?

When we talk about a pay per click (PPC) ad, we mean a search result—the four-line entry that will display on the results page in the area of the page called *Sponsored Links* in Google, *Sponsor Results* in Yahoo! and *Sponsored Sites* in MSN Live. The industry refers to these sponsored or paid search results as "text ads" (as distinguished from banner ads, pop-up ads, and other kinds of paid ads); Figure 10.1 shows what they look like.

Free Webber **BBQ Grill**
Just Complete 1 Offer & It's Yours
Free Webber BabyQ **BBQ Grill**
www.MyGrillOffer.com

Figure 10.1   **Example of a PPC Ad**

These ads consist of a one-line headline, two lines of text, and a web address. There are small variations among Google, Yahoo! and MSN, in general, the results look pretty much the same.

Sometimes the paid ads will display at the top of the page, sometimes on the side, and sometimes at the bottom. Their location varies depending on the search engine's algorithm. Figures 10.2 through 10.4 show how they might appear on each of the major search engines.

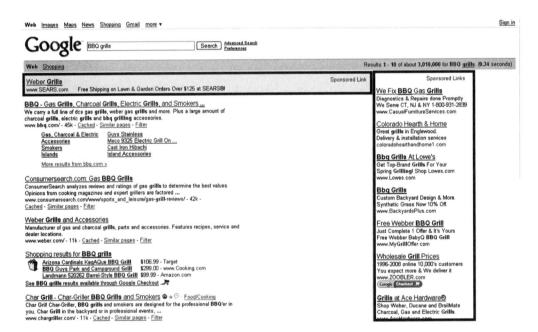

Figure 10.2   **Google Paid Search**

Google screenshots © Google Inc. Used with permission.

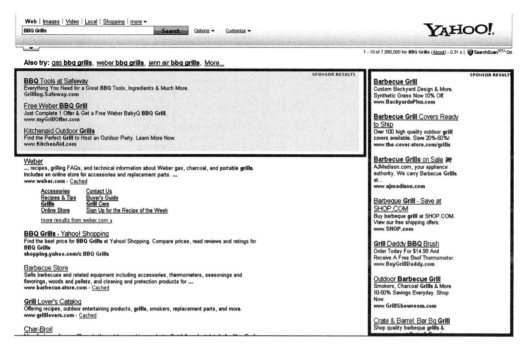

Figure 10.3   **Yahoo Paid Search**

Yahoo! Search Marketing. Used with permission.

How Hard Could It Be?

The task before you now is to write your own ads for your campaigns. You're probably looking at the preceding example and thinking—how hard could it be to write a four-line ad, or even a bunch of ads?

You'd be surprised.

The entire ad is only 95 characters—not *words*, mind you, *characters*. The top line allows 25 characters; the next two lines are 35 characters each, and then there's the display URL. That adds another 35 characters, and most of those are taken up by your web site address.

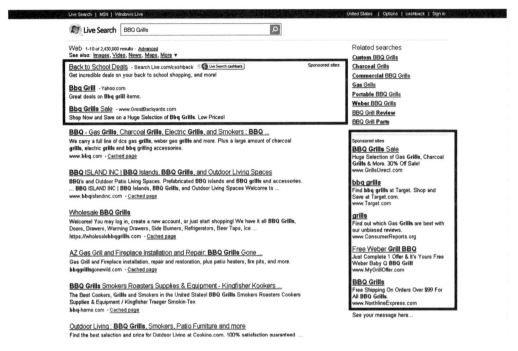

Figure 10.4   **MSN Paid Search**

MSN adCenter screenshots. Used with permission.

Yahoo! MSN, and Google have the same character limits on the descriptive lines of the ad—two lines of 35 characters each, or 70 characters.

It Ain't Easy

It's difficult to communicate a compelling message, generate interest, make a clear offer, stand out from the crowd, and make your ad keyword rich using only 70 characters. Writing paid search ads is an art that requires a fair amount of thought and effort. To write an ad effectively, you have to pare down your message, get right to the meat of the matter, and communicate in sound bites, not sentences. Leave out all filler words and all stop words (the, and, in, so, etc.). The payoff will come when the searcher chooses *your* ad to click on, and you have the opportunity to convert that searcher to a customer; so it's worth the effort.

Your Ad Writing Goals

What you're after is an *engaging* ad—well actually a few of them—that will tell searchers:

- Who you are
- What you are offering
- Why they should click on your ad text or visit your web page

You've got to make the ad **stand out on the page** and motivate the searcher to **click.**

Trust me—this can get frustrating. It's asking a lot of any marketer—and especially someone new to the world of search engine advertising—to convey critical messages in so few words. It may comfort you to realize that all your competitors have to do the same thing; and that doesn't really help you write your own ads.

However, *we're* going to help you.

Step 1: Ad Writing—Bucketed Keywords List

If you've followed the keyword recommendations up to this point, you should have a fairly robust list of 500 keywords or more.

Now you'll see the wisdom of bucketing and themeing your keywords list: you're not going to have to write ads for all 500

Table 10.1   **ABC Computer Company Keyword List**

Keywords	Bucket/Theme
Computer	Generic—old keywords
PC	Generic—old keywords
Gaming computer	Generic—old keywords
Gaming PC	Generic—old keywords
Quad Core gaming computer	Niche gaming
Nvidia Graphics computer	Niche gaming
Liquid Cooled computer	Niche gaming
ATI Radeon gaming computer	Niche gaming
Computer gaming world	High-volume gaming
Computer gaming	High-volume gaming
Computer gaming world magazine	High-volume gaming
Custom gaming computer	High-volume gaming
Ultimate gaming computer	High-volume gaming

Table 10.2   **Keyword Bucket Organization**

Generic/Old	Niche Gaming	High-Volume Gaming
Keywords: computer, PC, gaming computer, gaming PC	quad core gaming computer, Nvidia graphics computer liquid cooled computer, ATI radeon gaming computer	computer gaming world, computer gaming, computer gaming world magazine, custom gaming computer, ultimate gaming computer
Notes:	Notes:	Notes:
Ad:	Ad:	Ad
URL:	URL:	URL:
Destination:	Destination:	Destination

words. You're going to take your bucketed keywords, and you're going to *start with ONE ad for each bucket* or theme. While it may be tempting to write more ads for each theme, I'm a proponent of learning to walk before you run. So let's begin with one ad for each theme or bucket.

Let's say that the fictional ABC Computer Company's bucketed keywords list looks like Table 10.1.

In Table 10.2, we want to illustrate how each keyword bucket is organized. One ad is associated with each keyword bucket. Once you have organized your keywords in this fashion, you can begin writing one ad per keyword bucket.

Step 2: Understanding the Ad Text Landscape

Before you start composing your ads, look at the current results pages for your keywords to get a sense of what we call the "ad text landscape." You'd hate to spend a lot of time writing the perfect three-line, 95-word ad only to discover that it is identical to one of your competitor's ads or that what you thought was a brilliant offer *"free steaks with purchase of new gas grill"* was offered by every other gas grill seller on the page. Worse yet, you might realize that you omitted critical information (e.g., "free shipping"; "money-back guarantee") that you need to mention if everyone else is offering it.

Before you start writing, you need to know what you're up against and what you're shooting for. Because no matter what keyword strategy you choose, the bottom line is this:

If you want users to pay attention and click on your ad, you need to differentiate yourself from everyone else on the page.

Pick Me, Then Click Me

If you do not find a way to stand out, then you won't catch anyone's attention. You'll be like wallpaper that simply blends into the background, and that's exactly what you *don't* want. What you DO want is for your searchers to **notice you** as they're scanning the results and then to **click on your ad.** That is why we're going to have you look at the existing landscape for each keyword you've chosen.

You'll do this by typing in each of your top terms, hitting *search,* and then *scanning* the results that come up. Which ones catch your attention? Which ads have creative text or a compelling offer that grabs you? Which ones are you most drawn to and why? Do your scan quickly, as an actual user would on all three search engines—Google, Yahoo! and MSN—and see what "pops." Then print the results pages, and keep them for later reference.

The Components of a Paid Search Ad

Before you undertake the exercise we just assigned, it's good to understand what comprises a PPC ad. Here's a brief overview (we discuss this in detail later) of the components of a 4-line PPC text ad and the character limitations of each as depicted in Figure 10.5:

- **Headline:** 25 characters
- **Description Line 1:** 35 characters
- **Description Line 2:** 35 characters
- **Display URL:** 35 characters

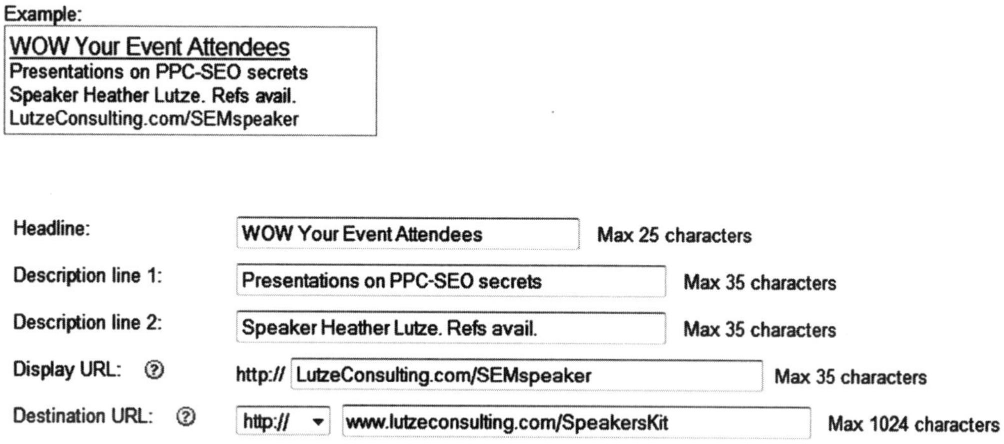

Example:

WOW Your Event Attendees
Presentations on PPC-SEO secrets
Speaker Heather Lutze. Refs avail.
LutzeConsulting.com/SEMspeaker

Headline: WOW Your Event Attendees   Max 25 characters

Description line 1:   Presentations on PPC-SEO secrets   Max 35 characters

Description line 2:   Speaker Heather Lutze. Refs avail.   Max 35 characters

Display URL: ⑦   http:// LutzeConsulting.com/SEMspeaker   Max 35 characters

Destination URL: ⑦   http:// ▼ www.lutzeconsulting.com/SpeakersKit   Max 1024 characters

Figure 10.5   **Example of PPC Ad Text Components**

Google screenshots © Google Inc. Used with permission.

A Window into Your Competitors' Souls

Since you're now armed with a basic understanding of what you're looking at, go check out the page one results for the terms you're using to run campaigns. Make notes for your own ads based on what you think works and what doesn't on those pages. Then, return to those pages and peruse them more slowly, with the mindset of a competitor rather than a searcher. Who is showing up under your chosen search terms? Are they your competitors? Are they the companies that you expected to be there?

Research everyone showing up in the top ad positions on Page One of your top search terms. Check them out from top to bottom and from front to back. Learn as much as you can about your competitors. If you're concerned about the ethics of clicking on your competitors' ads—when you know they're paying for that click, then the following advice will help you avoid "Bad Click Karma."

Ad Preview Tool

To operate as an honorable net citizen, you can use Google's **Ad Preview Tool** and see the ad text landscape for a given keyword. Google offers a handy way to look at keyword results without skewing ad statistics:

> **https://adwords.google.com/select/AdTargetingPreview Tool**

This ad preview tool is what I like to use when checking ads. This way, every time I (or the thousands of other advertisers) check on either keywords or ads, we are not skewing each other's data. This tool gives you an unbiased display of all the ads Google is currently displaying for a given keyword. Since Google attempts to provide customized user search results based on your prior search history, using the ad preview tool gives you an unbiased, non-personalized search result page by keyword with non-clickable ads.

This ad preview tool is also useful for checking your own ads. Advertisers need to be careful about how often they are pulling up their own favored keywords and must be careful to avoid taking action on those terms. The search engine will eventually interpret this as a non-relevant result for you because you are not clicking your ad text. Consequently, the search engine will stop displaying your own ad to you, and will give you the impression that your ads are not being displayed.

You are probably tempted to click on a few of your competitors' ads to see where they are sending searchers. You're also aware that the advertiser will be paying for those clicks, so you're not sure if it's okay to do that. My advice is to be considerate and judicious in using other advertisers' clicks; and also understand that it's a cost of doing business. Keep in mind, your competitors will probably also occasionally click on *your* ads to see what you're doing.

Putting Pen to Paper

Now, that you have sense of the landscape and the competition, you're ready to write your ads. Please keep the following points in mind:

- *Unique value proposition:* What do you have/offer that the others don't? What makes you the best choice on that page? Why should the searcher click on YOUR ad? Make sure that this information is crystal clear.
- *Positioning:* Remember the work you did at the very beginning of the keyword discovery process? Have your Positioning Statement nearby as you begin to write your ads, and make sure that they're consistent with who you are, and what you do—and don't do—as you compose your ad copy.
- *Offers:* Have your notes from your ad search with you. What were the other advertisers offering? If every ad on a page says "free shipping," then that's no longer any sort of differentiator or compelling offer. It's basically a non-offer because everyone is using it, and it doesn't add value or provide an incentive. Since it won't help you stand out or encourage a customer to click on your ad, you're going to have to come up with something else. If something like free shipping is critical, however, then you're going to have to also make room to add **"PLUS free shipping."**

> **WARNING**
>
> You cannot use trademarked names or words in your ad text. The search engines may flag that ad and withdraw it. While you can *bid* on trademarked terms, it may or may not make sense to do so if those keywords cannot appear in your ads. That's up to you. Absolutely *do not* include these terms in your ad text.

Those are general guidelines. Now let's break it down and walk through writing your ad, line by line.

The Headline

Purpose: **Hook 'em!**

The first line of the ad is the *Headline* also called the ad *Title*. This line displays as *underlined* because it's clickable. In Google, Yahoo! and MSN, the headline is limited to 25 characters. The headline's purpose is to grab users with a quick, one-line hook that immediately makes them want to read the rest of the ad. It should summarize what you are offering in the most succinct, compelling, and relevant terms. You should also try to include the ad theme/keyword in the headline if possible. Craft this text carefully because *it's your make-or-break opportunity to grab the searcher's attention.*

Let's move on from ABC Computer Company for this example and use the fictitious XYZ Gas Grill Company instead. We begin with an ad for their *gas grills* theme or bucket that will be displayed in response to a searcher typing in the term "gas grills." Keeping the buying cycle in mind, remember that a one- or two-word search term is pretty early in the customer's search, so the ads should be informational in nature, and not too hard-sell. An ad that says *"Weber E-320 Gas Grill On Sale NOW"* wouldn't be a good result because we know from the search term that the customer is not ready to buy and hasn't honed in on a brand yet (or we would be seeing the brand in the keyword phrase).

Here are some headlines that might meet gas grill searchers where they are in the search process and might get their attention.

Compare Quality Gas Grills

Compare = Informative

Expert Gas Grill Help

Expert = Learn from the pros

Huge Gas Grill Inventory

Inventory = Selection

These headlines attempt to tell the user what they will see if they click on the ads; and they're not trying to "sell" a grill. Notice that the keyword GAS GRILL is always used in the title.

You can also experiment with titles that are a little more creative or fun. They are not quite as clear about what searchers will see when they click; and they speak to their pain or desire, and they're clever. Searchers might well click on an ad that said:

Gas Grill Bliss

Bliss = Happiness

Headline is also funny = Fun

Dynamic Keyword Insertion

Another way to hook potential customers into clicking on your ad is to catch their eye with the ***exact keywords*** they just typed in. This is done by using something called *dynamic keyword insertion* (DKI), which is available as an option for any of your ad campaigns. This is an ingenious way of coding your ad title so that the search engine will automatically *insert the exact words* the user types into the search bar and *those words will appear as your ad title.* Since an ad that closely matches the search query equals better click rates and higher conversion rates, this is an extremely valuable technique. Not only does dynamic keyword insertion (DKI) make the title of your ad appear to be the exact search term the user just typed in, the keyword automatically **bolds** in your ad title and in your ad, drawing additional attention.

Let's say that the gas grill searcher types in "compare gas grills" and that you're using the dynamic keyword insertion instead of creating your own ad headline. What will come up with your ad—as the headline—will be:

Compare Gas Grills.

People like seeing their exact terms. They think it indicates the most relevant result.

If they type in:

"the best gas grills" your ad will show up with this headline:

The Best Gas Grills.

Although this is a great tool, it may not be appropriate for all situations. You may encounter circumstances wherein a majority of your competitors are already using the keyword insertion method in their ad text. In such a case, you would want to differentiate your ad from your competitors by NOT using keyword insertion so that your ad will stand out from the rest.

Bold Is Gold

In the search results, search engines automatically bold the keywords the user just typed in. Users see bold and know that bolded elements are highly relevant results that closely match their query. Indeed, it's what they are looking for. They aren't really reading search results pages; their eyes are *scanning* the results page for their keywords. By using dynamic keyword insertion, you are making your ad easier for the user to see—and also making it look more like a relevant search result (see Figure 10.6).

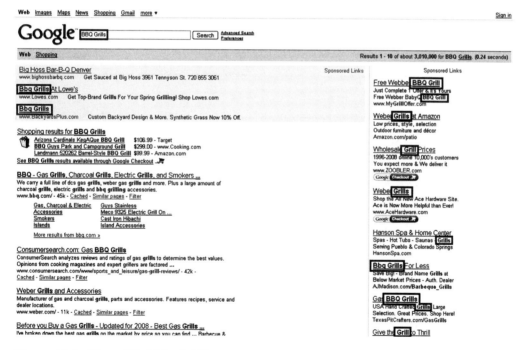

Figure 10.6 **Use of Bold in Ad Text**

Google screenshots © Google Inc. Used with permission.

DKI Tagging

Your ad title must be coded a specific way for the users' search terms to be inserted as such. You must bracket the word "keyword" in curly brackets followed by a colon to look exactly like this:

{**KeyW**ord: *Backup Keyword*}

One way to use dynamic keyword insertion is to type the word **KeyW**ord using capital letters for the first letter of each new word (which is known as "camel case") because this tells the engines to use initial caps when they insert the search phrase. (Don't use any spaces between words!) Having the keywords in initial caps makes the ad title look more professional. (*Gas Grills* looks better in a title than *gas grills*.)

Example

Wrong
Ad Text Title: {keyword: XYZ Gas Grills}
Searcher Types in: gas grills (18 characters)
Title as presented in Ad Text: gas grills

Note: Because "keyword" was not typed in camel case (mixed case) the results do not display with initial caps.

Right
Ad Text Title: {KeyWord: XYZ Gas Grills}
Searcher Types in: gas grills (18 characters)
Title as presented in Ad Text: Gas Grills

Note: By having 'KeyWord' in camel (mixed) case, the results display in initial caps.

For more information on Google's dynamic keyword insertion technique visit http://adwords.google.com/support /bin/answer.py?hl=en&answer=74996.

After the Colon: Your Backup Plan

After the {KeyWord} and the colon, you add a backup keyword. *Why do you add more content after the colon if the tag will insert the exact phrase anyway?* Sometimes users' search terms are longer than 25 characters. The limit for a title is 25 characters maximum, and you need to tell the search engine what to use in this instance. A good rule of thumb is that a generic or branding keyword or your domain name would all be excellent backup options.

The keywords after the colon are used when the search is more than 25 characters.

Ad Title in Account:	{KeyWord: XYZ Gas Grills}
Searcher Types in:	Viking Gas Outdoor Grills (27 characters)
Backup title displayed in search results:	XYZ Gas Grills

Since that about wraps up the headline overview, let's move on to writing the rest of the ad.

Description Line 1

Purpose: **To instill trust.**

The second line of an ad is where you present your company for the customer's consideration, and tell them why you are the best choice.

It's best to use quick, compelling words and phrases to keep the readers' attention, and to encourage them to keep reading for more information. Remember: ad text writing is done in chunks and sound bites, not complete sentences. Leave formality at the door. Come up with fun and creative ways to say who you are in a non-sentence format. Leave stop words out (and, and, the, to, it, etc.) if possible, and just stick to the facts.

The second line should also **tell searchers what they are going to see after they click on your ad**. This can include reviews, comparison charts, features, accessories, customer feedback, and any other relevant material. This makes your text look more like a search result than a paid ad.

As discussed, you have a maximum of 35 characters (including spaces) on this line to describe your product, service, offering, value proposition, or benefits (include your keyword again here if possible).

Examples of Copy for Description Line 1
- Huge Inventory, Free Freight
- Warehouse Selection, Talk to Expert
- 24/7 Help, Free Shipping
- Reviews & Customer Feedback

Description Line 2

Purpose: **What's in it for them?**

Line 2 provides another 35 characters to further explain your product or service and expand on what you mentioned in description line 1. Insert your keyword here if you did not include it in description line 1. Line 2 of your ad text is the place where you *have* to sell searchers with a reason or incentive and give them a quick idea of what they will get if they click on your ad: Free Shipping; Buy One, Get One; Free White Paper. Or, tell them what action you want them to take: book now, call now, order today. This is also where you get to describe—in a little more detail—exactly *what* you're offering and *why* your offer is better than anyone else's on the page.

Again, it's important to take the other ads into consideration, and to try to make yours interesting, fun, and unique. Don't imitate or duplicate the other ads. If everyone on the "gas grills" page is offering free shipping or free steaks (which most of them are), then come up with a better or distinctive offer.

We actually went to the gas grills page for this particular example, and noticed that no one was giving price points, a guarantee, or offering a phone number to call. To stand out, we thought it might be a good idea to mention a price and phone number, offer a guarantee, and/or offer some grilling assistance:

$399 and up. 888-555-1212
Cook Perfect Steak. Order Now.
45-Day Money-Back Guarantee
Talk to Grill Expert-888-555-1212

None of these were complicated or added a lot of text to our ad; however, they served to distinguish our ad sufficiently from that of the competition. Though we used a phone number in this example, keep in mind that using phone numbers in ads means searchers are likely to pick up the phone and call rather than click. While this does save you some money in click charges, it will also affect your click through rate, cost per click, and quality score. Use phone numbers judiciously and track these ads carefully.

Notes about Description Lines 1 and 2

Description lines 1 and 2 should each be a complete message. Let each one speak for itself as a whole. They should read like two distinct sound bite concepts. It is best to keep the message for line 1 in a single place, and to avoid carrying over onto line 2 (although sometimes you have no choice).

When you're done writing your title—as well as description lines 1 and 2—it's time to write your display URL; which isn't what you'd think at first glance.

The Display URL

Purpose: **Tell them again what you have to offer.**

Most people do not view the Display URL as a line of ad copy; however, those "in the know" do. The display URL (also called the *display domain*), is the most misunderstood line of a paid search ad, because it's sort of fake. Well, not fake exactly; it involves a bit of sleight of hand, because this line is not actually where your customer is going to be taken once they click.

The display URL *summarizes* the information that will be on the destination page (the page the ad will take searchers to if they click); however, it's not the actual address of the page. It *appears* to tell readers the URL of the page they're going to, where they will *actually* be taken is something you will be entering that the reader never sees.

If you understand that the display *URL is a summarization, not a destination,* you can use this line to your advantage to communicate your message or use your keyword one more time.

The display URL is like an additional line of free advertising in which you can communicate your message, reinforce your offer, and sell your product or service again.

Because so few advertisers know or understand this concept, they miss a perfect opportunity to have that one last chance to convince the user **"CLICK ME!"**

For the display URL in our gas grill example, you could enter a display URL that says something like this:

www.xyzGasGrills.com/**LowPrices**

I don't know about you, but I think I'd click on an ad that had "low prices" or some other offer as part of its web address—or at least what LOOKS like part of the web address.

Entering Your Display URL

The actual web address for the display URL must match the root domain of your destination URL, and you are limited to 35 characters including spaces.

You can enter your display URL in two ways: (1) put the keyword before the domain as a subdomain (prepend it) or (2) append it as a backslash keyword after the domain. They both look great on the ad and they still bold your keyword in the event that is what the searcher typed in the search box. It's all about using your search real estate to your fullest advantage.

Examples

1. Keyword appended after the URL
   a. YourDomain.com/**KeywordHere**
   b. GasGrills.com/**WeberGasGrills**
2. Subdomain keyword preceding URL
   a. **KeywordHere.**YourDomain.com
   b. **WeberGasGrills.**GasGrills.com

The Display URL is a great place to leverage your keywords one more time in the visible ad text area. This is also another opportunity for an additional bold element. You must work at enhancing every element of your ad text to differentiate your ad and your offer from your competitors.

The Destination URL

Purpose: **Don't make me think!**

This is where the click will actually take the user.

The destination URL is the real URL. It's the page you want the click to deliver your user to.

It has to be the exact address of the page including the http:// and the www—it's the full and precise URL of the web page you are taking the user to.

This line does not show up in your ad; *it is invisible to the user.*

The URL can be up to 1024 characters in length for Google and Yahoo! and up to 1022 for MSN. Therefore, you can be specific about where on your web site you want the user taken, or the specific address of your landing page. Although this many characters may seem long for a URL, there are deep databases and detailed page names that can be this long.

The customer, however, does not need or want to see that kind of complicated URL. Indeed, it might scare them away. The destination URL gives you the flexibility to drop them anywhere into your site without having to expose a complex URL. And they don't care what the address of the page is anyway.

They just want to be delivered to a good result.

The most critical thing you need to know about the destination URL is this:

For your paid search campaign to perform, you have to send users to a page that is totally relevant to the search term they entered and the ad they just clicked on.

It's up to the advertiser—you—to make sure they land on the most relevant page in relation to the search topic and the wording of the ad.

We devote an entire section to where the user should be taken for your campaign to succeed. Right now, let's focus on writing the four line ads you need for your chosen keywords. Work on your headline, two lines of description, and a clever display URL.

We cover the destination URL in detail later, and want to warn you now that it's critical to double-check that ALL your destination URLs are working BEFORE you turn on your campaigns. You don't want to pay for clicks to dead pages or think that your ads are running when they haven't been approved because of a broken link.

More Help with Ad Text

Now that you understand what's required of a text ad, you are probably asking yourself how the heck you're supposed to communicate what your business does and the unique value proposition you deliver in one 25-word headline, two lines of 35 characters each, and a display URL.

This task requires you to dismiss all normal marketing phrases. It forces you to use incomplete sentences and write in thought fragments. All extraneous words must be eliminated. You've got to get right to your point and get there fast.

Your message must basically deliver this information and nothing else:

- Here's why I showed up on this page.
- Here's what I offer/why you should pick me/why I'm the best result on this page.
- Here's what you'll get more of if you click.
- Here's what I'll deliver for your effort.

The ad also needs to clearly tie back to the keyword bucket for which you are writing the ad because you need to deliver a cohesive user experience.

We've broken down the components and walked you through it line by line; now let's work on an ad as a whole instead of in parts.

Real-Life Example

Using my own business as an example, let's say that I want to build the keynote-presentation-speaking side of my firm, and want to create and run an ad campaign solely for that.

1. The first step is to choose my bucket that I call "speaking keywords." Inside that bucket are the following keywords: Internet marketing speaker, Internet marketing presenter, search marketing speaker, search marketing presenter, search engine presenter.

2. My next task is to write my headline. If I'm not using dynamic keyword insertion, I need to choose a 25-character title. For this first ad, I am not going to get clever. I want something basic and straightforward. So I'm going with:

   Headline: *Search Engine Authority*

   That is my theme, my topic, and includes my keyword. The title also directly communicates what I'm offering.

3. Now I need to write my first description line. I want to make reference to the main topic of the ad, and I don't want to repeat it too much. I also want it to be a "good" and "relevant" search result, and provide clear information about what I do and who I am. I also want to establish credibility. My second line looks like this:

   Description Line 1: *Qualified Search Marketing Speaker*

4. My next descriptor needs to offer something unique. I was also able to sneak in a call to action.

Description Line 2: *Low Tech, Entertaining, Book Today!*

5. And now I want to deliver the message one more time in my display URL:

Display URL: *Speaker.LutzeConsulting.com*

Here's how the ad reads in its entirety:

Search Engine Authority
(Hook 'em.)
Qualified Search Marketing Speaker
(Trust me.)
Low Tech, Entertaining, Book Today!
(What's in it for them?)
Speaker.LutzeConsulting.com
(URL plus keyword one more time.)

This ad makes it clear that I'm a speaker on the subject of search engine marketing, a fact that that the title and description clearly state. Description line 1 gives me the opportunity to establish credibility and trust. Description line 2 informs searchers what they can expect if they engage me for their event, and the Display URL gives them the keyword "speaker" one more time.

Sometimes just one reference to the keyword is enough; it's going to be different for each business. And it's important that your ad not be generic. It must give the user a unique reason to click, a reason to choose you.

Remember, your goal is to create a good search result, so you have to find the balance between sales text and delivering a relevant result. A search engine is principally an information medium, not an advertising medium, and it's good to keep that in mind when writing your ads. Be sure that your ads always contain good *information* along with their unique value proposition, credibility, and compelling offers.

Trust

Online users trust search results.

The majority of searchers do not differentiate between sponsored (paid) ads and organic results. They believe that when they see your entry on a search results page, Google, Yahoo! or MSN has somehow given you its stamp of approval. They believe that the search engines are in essence saying to them, *Based on what you just typed in, the information that appears on this page is good information in response to your search request and will give you what you just asked for.*

Users believe that the displayed results are legitimate, relevant, and earned. Based on that assumption, your ad should be written as if the search engines personally selected you as being qualified to show up in their search results, and that they have recognized you as an authority in this arena.

If you don't write your ad with that in mind, then you're negating the authority, or the perceived authority, that the search engine has vested in you.

I know you're paying for the privilege of appearing on that page, and *you* know you're paying for it, and most non-technical, less-savvy searchers don't differentiate between paid search results and organic results. The illusion is that Google (or one of the others) *chose* you and that there's a reason you deserve to be on that page—you're a good search result. So your ad should be written in that vein.

Just as you need to remember that the searchers trust search engine results, and that they respond to relevant results, there's another principle to keep in mind as you sit down to write your ads:

A search engine is not an advertising medium; it's an information medium.

I know we previously told you to write your ad so that it conveys your unique value proposition and makes a compelling offer and now we seem to be saying "tone down the advertising aspects of your ad"; however, we're just asking you to temper your ad text with this understanding:

People do not conduct online searches to see advertising.

No one approaches a search engine looking for ads. Of course, hardly anyone is actually *looking* for ads—ever. You're not tuning in to find promotions when you watch TV, read newspapers or magazines, or listen to the radio. You're there to hear music or read the news for information or entertainment, and ads are the necessary evil. In fact, that's why digital recording devices like TiVo have become so popular; people don't like commercials. They want to get what they came for: information, entertainment, or whatever it may be.

The same is true of search engines; people come to them for information. Your job is to guide them to the *information* they just asked for. If there are ads at the top or at the side, users will tolerate them if they have to. And since what they are truly seeking are search results, these should read more like relevant material and less like advertising or marketing.

Ideally, the paid ads should blend into the search results. As the users scan over the page, they should evaluate your ad with the same trust as all the other results (paid and unpaid) on the page. A hard-core sales ad runs the risk of being dismissed and disqualified by a searcher as an untrustworthy result. Ignoring this principle is a common mistake that advertisers make in their paid search campaigns. Although you want your ad to "pop," you also want the marketing aspect of it to be understated.

The Italian Job versus *Wayne's World*

Your "product placement" will be there, and try to make it subtle. Think about the movie *The Italian Job*. They never mention the Mini Cooper car, and after watching that movie, everyone wants one.

Contrast that with *Wayne's World,* when in the middle of a scene, Wayne turns to the camera and says—apropos of nothing—"Pepsi, the choice of a new generation!" He was satirizing product placement in a jarring and disruptive way. Nothing about it feels natural or organic; it was totally inappropriate (although that was probably the intention). Your job is to make your ad feel like a natural and entirely pertinent response to a search query.

Keeping this principle of *information, not advertising* in mind is particularly important when working with the buying cycle—especially in the earliest stage of the buying cycle when users are searching for information above all else.

Incorporating the Buying Cycle into Your Ad Campaign

The best way to incorporate the buying cycle into your ad campaign is to put yourself in your prospects' shoes.

If you are working on a particular bucket—let's say you sell TVs and you're working on your "Plasma TV" bucket—ask yourself, *If I just typed in "plasma TV 14 inch," what search results would I want to see? Do I want an ad that is selling me a television or am I hoping for an informational ad telling me "this is the next step you should take in your path" or "here are the brands to consider and how they stack up?"*

This is where the concept of different keywords for different parts of the buying cycle really comes into play. Ask yourself: *What are the informational keywords, the shopping keywords, the buying keywords for this search*—and then craft ads that will appropriately speak to your customer at exactly where he or she is in the buying cycle.

Remember that the keywords users type in let you know where they are on their path, and enable you to tailor your ads.

Plasma 14-inch is a *shopping* keyword. The length of that string and the criteria included tell us that the searcher is starting to hone in on what he or she wants. The person is still shopping and getting closer to purchasing.

The appropriate question to ask in this phase of ad writing is: *If this customer is shopping for a 14 inch plasma TV, what is it that he or she wants and needs right now? What will be most helpful and most useful?*

Probably, this searcher would find information about the best brands for 14-inch plasma TVs the most helpful result. If this customer had typed in "new TVs" you'd want to provide education about all the kinds of TVs available, such as plasma, flat screen, high def, and rear projection. You would want to communicate: *My company can be trusted to guide you through this confusing world.*

If searchers are typing in a keyword string with a brand name, size, and specifications, then they're ready to buy and want to know the best deal, warranty, perks, and delivery terms.

You get the picture; now let's walk through a path-to-purchase ad writing exercise.

Ads along the Path to Purchase

Example 1

Search Term: *TV*
Search Phase: Information/Research

TV is an informational search term, so you would want to write an ad that speaks to assisting the user in his or her search and positions you as a resource for that activity.

Ad Example

Title: *Looking for a New TV?*
Line 1: Start Here for Huge Selection
Line 2: TV Experts 24/7—Low Price Leader
Display URL: Expert-TV-Help.xyzcompany.com

Example 2

Search Term: *Sony plasma television*
Search Phase: Shopping

This three-word string is a shopping keyword. These searchers are telling us that they know what type of TV they want and also what brand. They've moved down the purchasing cycle, and are now looking for a search result that helps them choose model, size, and features. They want a Sony Plasma TV and are asking themselves: *which model is right for me?* So you'd want to position yourself as the quintessential guide to choosing the right Sony plasma TV for their needs.

Ad Example

Find Sony Plasma TVs
All Models. Great Prices.
TV Experts 24/7—Get Sony Here.
Huge-TV-Selection.xyzcompany.com

Example 3

Keyword: Sony plasma television 72" Denver
Search Phase: Purchasing

This search string tells us that the customer has done his or her research and shopping, and is now ready to buy. The credit card is out and at the ready. This customer has identified type, brand, size, and the location for the purchase. Now you want to craft an ad that says: *"We are the largest Sony plasma television supplier in the United States. We ship anywhere in the U.S. for free. We offer a lifetime guarantee,* and so forth. What you want this ad to do is reassure them that you are the best company to buy from even if you're not in their city. Let them know you'll get them their TV for free and the shipping to Denver is guaranteed.

You probably also want to mention that you have a great selection. Let them know you're their Internet resource for great prices and guaranteed delivery for Sony TVs. At this point, do everything you can to reassure the customer that this is where they need to buy. You want to give them reasons to buy from you if you are not in Denver. Let them know you get where they are. You get their concerns. You're ready to help them and get them their new TV. *They can be happily watching their new Sony plasma soon.*

At this point in the process, if you give searchers a generic televisions ad, you are NOT going to get their business. A highly targeted ad that speaks directly to where they are in the buying cycle has a pretty good chance of getting them to click on the purchase page. And that's what you want. Maybe you can even provide an incentive with free DVDs or some other offer that will entice them to *BUY NOW.*

Here's an example:

Denver's Sony TV Source
Free Shipping Low Price Guarantee
Buy Today, Watch Tomorrow. Act Now.
SonyPlasma.xyzCompany.com

Different products and services have different paths to purchase. High-end and low-end offerings have separate paths, as do high price points and low price points. A $20 lamp has a much shorter path to purchase than a $2,000 television or a $20,000 car. They still have the same stages: *information, shopping, and purchasing,* and you still need to know what to say to the customer at the right time.

Failing to do this is one of the most common errors we see. Advertisers often provide informational ads to purchasing searchers, or purchasing ads to informational searchers or shopping searchers.

They want to get the customer to BUY; however, they're running an informational keyword like "television" in their campaign and they're pushing for a purchase too soon in the cycle. This creates a disconnect for the customer, and that customer moves on.

Run informational ads for your information keywords, shopping ads for your shopping keywords and purchasing ads for your purchasing keywords. That's what we mean by *properly targeted campaigns.*

Don't waste your money paying for clicks when you are not in sync with what the customer wants and needs at that moment; neither you nor they will get the desired result.

Typically a paid search ad geared to the wrong purchasing stage shows up as lots of clicks on the ad, and very few conversions. If you've been running ads that have you scratching your head and asking: *Why am I getting all these clicks, and no one is taking action?* Chances are there is incongruence between where the customer is in the buying cycle and what you're providing.

You must pay attention to what the *keyword* is communicating, and then appropriately speak to the customer at each stage of the purchasing path. Understanding the relationship between keywords and the ads you present in response to them is critical to a successful paid search campaign. Being there with the right information at the right time makes the difference. Don't run a "buy now" ad for a generic, informational keyword like television. Don't tell searchers you carry every brand of TV when they've clearly told you they're looking for a *14-inch Sony plasma TV*.

Okay, now the ball is in your court. Write your ads. Write one for each keyword bucket.

If you feel it's important, you can write more than one ad for each ad group to test performance; however, be careful not to take on more than you can handle. You can always experiment with different ad texts later.

Take-Aways

- Ad writing requires creative thinking. You have only four short lines to get your message across and to make it stand out on a results page.
- Use the display URL as an additional marketing message.
- Study your competition on the keyword results pages before writing your own ads.
- Make sure you use your keywords in the ad.
- Use compelling text that reads more like a "search result" than an advertisement.
- Keep the buying cycle or date specific events in mind when writing ads.
- Learn to use dynamic keyword insertion for your ad headlines and/or descriptions when appropriate.
- Make sure your destination URL is the most relevant page you can send the searcher to in your site.

Tools You Use in This Chapter
- Google AdPreview Tool, https://adwords.google.com/select/AdTargetingPreviewTool
- Dynamic Keyword Insertion, http://adwords.google.com/support/bin/answer.py?hl=en&answer=74996

CHAPTER 11

After the Click

Before you launch your pay per click (PPC) campaign, you have to plan precisely where their "click" will take your customers for each ad.

For three reasons, this ranks as high in importance as everything else we've covered to this point:

1. If you send customers to a page that isn't what they wanted or expected, they will be annoyed and frustrated . . . and GO AWAY. You will lose them.
2. You just PAID for a click that isn't going to serve you (or the customer); *that is totally wasted money.*
3. The relevance of the page they land on (landing page) affects the *quality score* that the search engines assign, which in turn will affect your ranking and placement on the results page as well as the cost of your ad.

What is quality score? I am glad you asked because that is exactly what the next section is about.

Quality Score

Quality Score is a rating that search engines assign to every keyword in your account **based on the sum total of the user experience,** including your ad text and the page you take them to.

Quality Score—also called Quality Index—is critical because it affects your placement on a page, and also **how much you pay** to be displayed in the PPC results. If you have a great quality score, you can potentially pay less for a higher position on the page than your competitors might pay for lower positions.

These scores can also be good feedback about the search experience and can help you tweak your alignment with the searchers intention for each searched keyword.

Most important is that the quality of your ad and the page to which you take searches will affect the bottom line performance of your ad campaign. These are all good reasons why you should care about quality.

The search engines also care about quality. They care very much about the *relevance and quality* of search results because their entire business model and reputation depend on it. The more you provide relevance and quality in the user experience, the more the search engines (and searchers!) will like you and reward you.

In a nutshell, quality score is the relevance of your keywords to your ad text and your ad text to your landing page copy.

Here are Google, Yahoo! and MSN adCenter official quality score descriptions at the time of publication:

Quality Score for Google Definition

"Quality Score for Google and the search network is a dynamic metric assigned to each of your keywords. It's calculated using a variety of factors and measures how relevant your keyword is to your ad group and to a user's search query. The higher a keyword's Quality Score, the lower its minimum bid and the better its ad position."

Source: http://adwords.blogspot.com/2007/02/quality-score-updates.html.

Quality Index Yahoo! Search Marketing Definition

The quality index is a relative measure of how relevant an ad is. It reflects an ad's ability to meet the needs of users by taking into account various relevance factors and click-through rate compared to its position and other ads displayed at the same time. It also takes into account all keywords in your ad group.

Source: http://help.yahoo.com/l/us/yahoo/ysm/sps/start/overview_qualityindex.html.

Quality Score MSN adCenter Definition

As of the publication date of this book, MSN adCenter has Quality Score in a beta test for select advertiser accounts. Look for this feature to become available for all users in the coming months. Keep checking the adCenter Help site for updated information.

Source: http://tinyurl.com/MSNAdCenterHelp.

What You Need to Know

What you need to take from those definitions and what you need to pay the most attention to is:

- **Your Click Through Rate (CTR):** That is, how many people choose to click on your ad
- **Your Bid:** What you are willing to pay for the search term
- **The Quality and Relevance of Your Landing Page for your customers**

Although an entire blog is devoted to the hotly debated subject of the elements of the quality score—http://adwords.blogspot .com/2007/02/quality-score-updates.html—frankly, you could drive yourself crazy trying to keep up with all the components that go into the scoring.

If you stay focused on the **customer experience,** you will maximize your quality score *and* increase conversions. This will not only improve your sales, it will also further improve your score.

The bottom line is that your quality score is dependent on the user experience.

As such, I advise my clients: *Pay attention to your customers,* not so much on quality score or quality index. Deliver a relevant result and an excellent customer experience, and you will win the quality score game.

We'll show you how to check your Quality Score in Chapter 14—Checking Your Quality Score. Once your campaigns are up and running, for now we need to focus on the element of the user experience (and quality score) that deals with *where searchers will be taken to once they click on your ad.*

Where Are You Sending Them?

The most common mistake that advertisers make at this stage of the game is driving all their paid search ads to their web site home page. After all, it's the main page, right? It tells who you are and what you do, right?

Well, sometimes, right. And very often, *wrong.*

Because what you want to do is send them to the MOST RELEVANT page on your site. Yes, we have said this a hundred times; however, since it is *the single most important thing that has to happen now,* we're saying it again.

Once customers have clicked on your ad, that click needs to deliver them to the closest possible match to the topic/keyword they just searched.

If they've asked for plumbing supplies and you deliver them to the main page of a *Construction Materials* web site, they're not going to be happy. They already told you they're looking for *plumbing supplies;* maybe they even told you they need *1 inch copper pipe,* why should they have to tell you again? Why should they have to search the page for the link to plumbing supplies?

That's a bad user experience and they're likely to be frustrated and leave the site pretty quickly. You just paid for a worthless click, frustrated a searcher, and damaged your quality score. A bad result on three fronts.

Nobody wants that.

Do this instead:

- Take the *plumbing supplies* searcher to the plumbing supplies page.
- Take the *1 inch copper pipe* searcher to the page that displays your 1 inch copper pipe.

What your customers are telling you about where they are in the buying cycle and what they want and need from you at this moment should determine where you take them on your web site or landing page.

If the searcher is typing in general, information-gathering key-words, then a higher level overview page—that your home page probably provides—might be fine.

For searchers typing shopping or purchasing keywords into the search box, it's critical to be mindful of the answers to these questions:

- Where is the **best place on my site** for them to land?
- Where do I have *content with the closest match to the interest they've expressed in their search query?*

The answer to these questions is where that click should take them.

If they indicated *Sony televisions,* you should take them to a Sony page or a manufacturer's comparison page (e.g., how does Sony compare to JVC, Toshiba, and Magnavox). This is probably not your home page.

If they've typed in *plasma resolution* or *flat panel resolution,* then your best result is to take them to a page that addresses technical specifications.

And if they're typing in *Sony TV* with a specific size and model number, then they're telling you that they're ready to buy . . . so take them to the order page for that product.

Bottom line:

For a great quality score, high customer satisfaction, and consistent conversions, you must take your customers where they've clearly told you they want to go.

By paying attention to what searchers are communicating with their keywords, taking them to your web site at the exact point of interest they've indicated, and exactly where they are in their buying cycle, you've created a very satisfying user experience.

This exponentially increases your chances of a conversion from that visit. It also improves your quality score.

By reading and responding to the signals the searcher is communicating and directing them accordingly, you will be rewarded with your visitor's desired behavior. And an improved quality score.

Notice the focus is on the visitor experience, and quality score is the by-product. That's the right focus for all your search marketing.

Ad Correlation

The result visitors see—the page you take them to—should be directly correlated to their search phrase, and also to the text (content) of the PPC ad they just clicked.

It should match the ad topic as closely as possible, without any disconnect or lack of continuity.

If you think about the ad we wrote for *search marketing speaker*, you will understand the importance of that ad landing on the page of my site that is specifically about my *speaking and keynotes*. If that ad went to my home page, visitors would get there and go "huh?"

because the *ad* they just clicked on was talking about speaking and presentations not search marketing consulting, which is what my home page addresses.

Maybe they would find the button that says *Speaking and Keynotes* and click on that, or *maybe* they would just leave. And who would blame them? They were clear about what they were asking for, clear about their interest, and I didn't pay attention and respond accordingly. If I don't take them to their requested destination, do I deserve their business?

For a good result, it is my job to take them to the page my site on the *Speaking and Keynotes* page. That is my responsibility as an advertiser.

Brick-and-Mortar Metaphor

Imagine walking into a store and looking for a one-piece woman's swimsuit in response to an ad you saw in the paper. You ask the first person you see to direct you to the bathing suits, and the salesperson sends you to the main women's clothing area. There, you ask again, "Where can I find one-piece swimsuits?" This time, you're directed to women's sportswear. You have to ask yet again, and this time, someone points you toward the swimsuits . . . and it's a rounder rack of *two-piece* suits. So you have to find someone and ask again, or wander around yourself until you find what you're looking for. *This is a bad and frustrating user experience.*

Contrast that scenario with walking into a store, ad in hand, asking for one-piece swimsuits and being personally escorted directly to the rounder of one-piece suits, with the clerk graciously telling you, "Here are all our one piece swimsuits, in a variety of colors and patterns. I believe this is exactly what you were asking for."

See the difference? *Feel* the difference? ***That's*** what you're after for your customer's online experience.

Your customers clearly tell you what they're interested in by the keywords they use in their search. So, deliver a relevant result to them with **both your ad and where you take them once they've clicked.** It's the only way to succeed with pay per click marketing.

In a brick-and-mortar store, a customer who is already there is less likely to leave even if the experience isn't satisfying. This is not the case on the Internet—where the next "store" is just a click away.

Decide on the right page for each ad. The address of that page is what you will enter into the **Destination URL** blank on your ad spreadsheet (which will later be uploaded to the search engine).

Uh-Oh

What if you don't have a super-relevant page on your web site? What if your site is four years old and you've been meaning to get around to updating it and haven't had the time or can't afford that update right now?

You have three viable options:

1. Scratch that particular campaign, because a bad user experience is just going to frustrate your prospect and waste your money.
2. Create a relevant web page in your existing site.
3. Create a *landing* page specifically designed for your prospects to land on after they click; it should speak directly to your specific campaign or offer, and is not necessarily linked to your current web site.

Landing Pages

A *landing page* is a page you create specifically as the destination for searchers who click on a PPC ad. It is designed to directly correlate with the message of the ad and to focus searchers' attention on the specific action you want them to take.

You have a few seconds once they've arrived on a page to convince the visitor to take action. A landing page is one way to make the most of that time.

If you take searchers to your home page—or another page on your web site that isn't action-focused, you have less ability to direct or control their behavior. Landing pages communicate a clear action-oriented message and generally provide an incentive or some other encouragement for visitors to take the action you want them to take (e.g., fill out a form, download a white paper, view a video, or purchase a product).

Landing pages are written with a message that identically matches the searchers' keyword phrase and the ad text.

After they have landed, visitors feel they've received a response/result that is super relevant to their search, which in turn increases the chances of a conversion *that is, the visitor taking the desired action.*

Since, as a PPC advertiser, you are *paying for every click,* you want the most valuable response and best return on your investment. By directing your visitor to take action, landing pages can help deliver that response.

Landing Page Overview

A detailed course on landing pages is outside the scope of this book; however, here's a quick primer:

- The purpose of a landing page is to be focused, specific, and relevant, while speaking directly to a need that's been expressed.
- Usually a landing page has a specific call to action. The subtext is "We've delivered you to the perfect page and given you exactly what you asked for, now make a decision!" As such, landing pages tend to be conversion oriented.
- They often include a unique incentive or offer designed to directly compel the desired action.
- A landing page bypasses your core site and takes the visitor to a specific page themed by keyword or keyword topic.
- These specially created landing pages are rarely connected to your web site; they're just sort of "orphans" out there in cyberspace (which is why they're also called *orphan landing pages*).
- Landing pages are designed to control what visitors see, where they go, and what you want them to do. Because of that, they often don't have navigation options. The thinking on this is that, with no navigation, there are no distractions or other reasons for the visitor to NOT take action. This feature of landing pages is a strongly debated topic.

To Navigate or Not to Navigate

A hotly contested argument in landing page testing is whether to include navigation on these pages. Obviously, the more options you give visitors to NOT take action, the more they will avoid it. My advice to clients is to test this theory carefully. Create two identical landing pages, one with navigation links back to your home page and one without any navigation. Test both and see which landing page converts more customers. This will solve the debate for your business. Don't guess, test.

Landing Page Uses

In addition to using a landing page when you don't have a closely relevant page on your site to correlate to your ad campaign, or you want a specific action-oriented page, you can have landing pages for short-term, event-specific, or seasonal offers:

- You might create a landing page for a convention with an offer directed at convention customers. The person who clicks on an ad related to convention opportunities is not interested in the breadth of your services as outlined on your web site. They're interested in one specific thing: what you're offering at the convention. Anything else would be a distraction.
- Another example might be that this year, the whitewater is flowing like crazy in Colorado; many are calling it the highest water we've had in a long time. It would be a mistake for a rafting company to tout this on its main web site because it could be over in a month; however, it might be a good use of a landing page to run a short-term ad campaign saying, "The best whitewater in years." It should land on a page specifically created for and geared to that message, with a clear *"make reservations now before the water recedes"* call to action.

You can probably think of numerous examples of seasonal, focused, or short-term offers or sales where landing pages would be an appropriate marketing tool. In general, a landing page is the perfect way to deliver a singular focus on a particular offering.

Landing Page Caution

Landing pages are not built for search engines. They are built specifically for PPC and ***should not be indexed.*** Make sure your web designer understands this because *otherwise a landing page can hurt your web site rankings.*

To ensure this does not happen, say these specific words to your web designer or IT person: "Make sure I have a 'no index' tag in the robots.txt file for my pay per click landing pages."

Let's skip the technical explanation, basically you are telling your web designer or IT person to add a robots.txt file onto your landing page directory that alerts the search engines. This is just a page for visitors, not for search engines; **you don't want the search engines to index these pages.**

Checking Your Landing Page

For your ad campaign to be successful, visitors must have a relevant experience after they click on your ad. Whether you land them on the most appropriate page on your web site or create a special landing page for your campaign, where you send them is critical to your success. A good result will increase your conversions, your quality scores, and your page rankings.

One you've written your ads for each theme, enter the URL of the destination page you have chosen in the Destination URL cell of your spreadsheet. Next, put yourself in the shoes of your visitor, read your ad, and then visit the destination page you've chosen. If that page gives you good, satisfying, and relevant information in clear alignment with the keyword theme and the text of the ad, you're good to go.

If where you land is off-topic, confusing, or frustrating in any way, change the destination or create a relevant page as a landing page for that specific ad.

Otherwise, you are wasting money because your ad success depends on the user experience after the click.

Landing Page Guides and References

For in-depth information about landing pages and strategies, check out one of the many landing page reference guides and resources available. I particularly recommend these:

- 2008 *Landing Page Handbook* pricey at $497.00 plus shipping, available at MarketingSherpa.com and worth the money for an in depth review—http://www.sherpastore.com/product.php?ID=363
- *Landing Page Optimization: The Definitive Guide to Testing and Tuning for Conversions Book* by Tim Ash, http://www.landing-page-optimization-book.com
- *Google Landing Page Optimization Guide*—Very helpful, I've posted this on The Findability Formula web site at http://www.FindabilityFormula.com/landingpage

Take-Aways

- Where the searcher lands after clicking on your ad will, in large measure, determines the outcome of that click.
- The more relevant the page, the better your chances of a conversion.
- If the page is not what your searchers asked for or expected, they will simply leave.
- The relevance of the destination also affects the *quality score* that each search engine assigns, which in turn affects ad placement and even the price of your ads.
- If you're delivering search results that don't correlate with your keywords and ad text, you might be wasting searchers' time and your money.

Tools You Use in This Chapter
- Google Quality Score, http://adwords.blogspot.com/2007 /02/quality-score-updates.html
- Yahoo! Search Marketing Quality Index, http://help.yahoo .com/l/us/yahoo/ysm/sps/start/overview_ qualityindex.html
- MSN adCenter Quality Score Beta, http://tinyurl.com /MSNAdCenterHelp

CHAPTER 12

Bidding and Budgeting

You've brainstormed and built out your keywords, grouped them by theme, written ads, and figured out what landing page to send visitors to; however, before you're ready to deploy your pay per click (PPC) ad campaigns, you probably want to know how much this advertising will cost.

How Much Do PPC Ads Cost?

It is a legitimate question. Unfortunately, there's no easy answer. Finding out how much your ads will cost (per click) depends on the cost of the keywords you choose. And finding out the cost of your keywords requires going through several steps because *there are no set prices for keywords.*

You pay for keywords by bidding on them. And figuring out the bidding price range requires multiple steps.

When I explain this to clients—that we really can't know prices yet—they always get a little frustrated and impatient. And they all ask me if I can at least give them an estimate.

When I say "not really," usually they insist I give them something.

So I say, "okay, the price range for a keyword can run anywhere from as little as $0.01 to as much as you are willing to spend per keyword."

At that point, they usually roll their eyes . . . as if they think I'm being evasive. And I'm not. To prove it, I show them an example. We take a keyword like *mortgage,* and we look it up.

And what we find is that that term can run anywhere from $1.00 to $25.69 (source: Spyfu.com at time of book publication) per click, depending on:

- Where the advertiser wants to be on the page (position).
- How competitive (popular) the keyword is.
- How many advertisers are bidding on it.
- Where the advertiser runs it (geographic limitations).
- How long the keyword string is (usually the longer and more specific, the less money, but not always).
- And later on, your price will also depend on the "quality score" that the search engines assign as a result of the user experience with your ads.

That's why it's so hard to pin down price.

And of course you need to know. Because if you have a list of 500 keywords, and an average of 20 keywords in each ad group, you may not be able to afford to run all your campaigns from the start, depending on what the campaigns will cost. You need to know: *"Which of the ad groups that I've built in my campaigns can I afford to launch right out of the gate?"*

And to make this determination, you need to know the price of your keywords.

From the work you did with your keyword research tool, you already know your top-performing keywords, and figuring out what those terms cost is not as easy as simply "looking up the price" of each keyword:

- Every keyword has a different price from every other keyword depending on:
  — **Popularity/frequency of searches:** A popular keyword like *iPod,* which is frequently searched, costs more than a keyword like *Sony Walkman,* which probably isn't searched quite as often.
  — **How competitive the keyword is:** How many other advertisers also want that term (supply and demand)?
  — **The keyword phrase:** The price is also affected by the length of the keyword phrase; broader terms usually cost more, and longer and more specific terms cost less, and there are many exceptions.
- Within each keyword, there are no set prices. There are bid *ranges.* These ranges can vary widely, depending on several factors:
  — **Page position:** *Where* the advertiser wants to appear in sponsored search results will affect the price the advertiser pays. Top position costs the most. Top Three is pricier than Bottom Five, and so on. With an average of approximately 10 paid results on a page, advertisers must decide where they want to be and how much they are willing to pay for

their desired position. Just like any other bidding situation, the price will depend on how many people are bidding and how much they're willing to pay.

— **Geographic area:** It costs more to have your ad seen by the whole country or the whole state than just in your city or town.

Keyword pricing is also affected by:

— **Quality rating:** Once you've run your campaigns for a while, your bid price will depend on the quality score that the search engines assign based on the *users' experience* from the time they type in the keyword until they land on your page.

Although we've talked extensively about the importance of the user experience in terms of your *results,* and your placement on the page, your quality score also directly affects your *pricing.* Bottom line: if searchers like you, the search engines will like you and you will pay less for your keywords.

Despite all the variables that affect keyword pricing, you obviously still need to figure out *approximately* what a given keyword will cost you. Here's how you do that.

Research Your Keywords in SpyFu

SpyFu (http://www.SpyFu.com) is an invaluable tool for looking at the competitive nature of your keywords (see Figure 12.1). It is a *free and subscription-based* tool that enables you to enter a keyword and get the approximate bid range of that term as well as some other pertinent information such as number of advertisers, clicks per

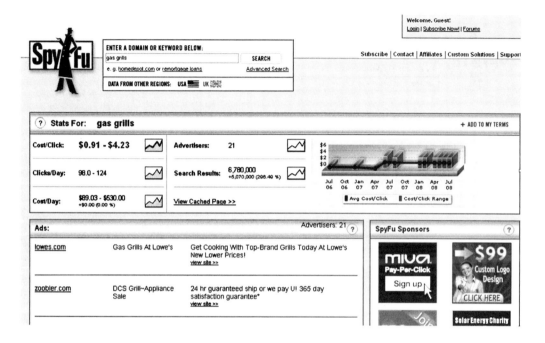

Figure 12.1 **SpyFu**

Spyfu.com. Used with permission.

day, search results, cost per day, ad text, and additional keywords advertisers are already bidding on.

If you type "gas grills" into the home page search box of SpyFu, it will show you that the cost/click of "gas grills" would range from $0.91 to $4.23 per click depending on where you want to appear on the page.

If you want top position, and $4.23 is a little rich for your blood or you want a more targeted, narrower term, you might try "outdoor gas grills" as an alternative (see Figure 12.2). Because that is a narrower term with fewer people bidding on it (which is another reason we had you narrowly target your terms), "outdoor gas grills" will cost you only $0.45—$1.21 per click—one half to one-third the price.

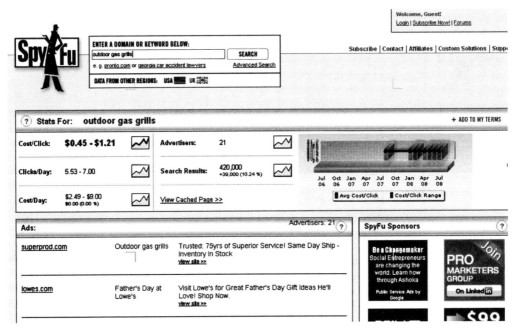

Figure 12.2   **SpyFu Outdoor Gas Grills**

Spyfu.com. Used with permission.

If you entered a brand name, it would probably narrow the competition even more and probably cost even less. Although not always. If it's a particularly hot brand, it might be more competitive than the generic term. That's why you have to run your terms through this tool to find out.

Obviously, you're not going to do this for all 500 of your keywords. Investigate your most competitive terms first.

You pick a term, you look at the range. If gas grills is too broad a term and too expensive, try outdoor gas grills. If that's still too much, try *discount gas grills* or *luxury gas grills* or *small gas grills* or whatever terms are narrower and more defined for your product or service. *See where the terms start to get affordable for you.*

Start with your informational terms and see where the prices are. Then take your longer tail keywords and see what prices come up. Check your keywords with brand-names and geographic modifiers. Because you have your ads conveniently grouped and themed, you can go through this exercise with relative ease. Maybe you can't afford gas grills, and if you narrow it to your area, you'll find that *gas grills Memphis* is right in the price range you were hoping for. Great, start with that ad group. Later you can broaden your reach and include higher-priced terms. You're just trying to figure out where you're starting point is and what you can afford.

This is a lot like pricing any other purchase you would make. You evaluate the price, what you are getting for that price, and how it fits into what you can afford in your overall budget.

Evaluation

If you were thinking $20/day ($600/mo) as a budget for an outdoor gas grills ad and first position was going to cost you $1.21 per click, that's only 16 clicks per day before your budget would be depleted. Is it worth it? Can you afford that? Is that a good use of your money? Do you need a bigger budget? Can you settle for a lesser position than number one? How much is top three? Still too much? Should you pick a more targeted and lower priced keyword, maybe a purchasing term rather than an informational term?

If your budget is $150/month ($5.00 a day) and your top-choice keyword is in the range of $2.50 per click, you can receive only two clicks a day. This choice is probably not worth the cost at this budget. Could your $5.00 be better spent on a more targeted term that's maybe only $0.25 per click and you could get in front of 20 people a day? And what if your research shows you that only about 20 people per day shop for that highly targeted term? Now your

$5.00 gets you in front of just about every searcher for that keyword, and it's a purchasing term to boot. That's probably a good buy—a wise advertising "spend."

These are the questions you will ask yourself as you gather bid data from SpyFu.

You want to start with a compelling bid that will keep you online a majority of the day, and will get you in front of the highest possible percentage of daily searchers. That's why you run your terms through SpyFu. You research relative costs so you can make intelligent decisions about how and where to spend your money.

In this stage, you are deciding which terms to go for, how much they're worth to you, and what you want to spend so that you can determine what you're going to bid for each keyword.

Only you can make these evaluations and determinations depending on your budget, the number of keywords on your list, the pages it's critical for your ad to appear on, the number of search engines you're running campaigns in, and so on.

You might also need to reassess your budget.

Bidding with the Buying Cycle in Mind

When evaluating which keywords to bid on, remember to look at your buying cycle buckets.

The more competitive the keyword landscape, the more expensive your keywords will be per click; and normally, the broader the term, the more expensive it is.

This is one reason this book spends so much time focusing on your customer's path to purchase and differentiating informational and shopping keywords from purchasing keywords. If you have a preponderance of expensive informational keywords in your campaign, then you are spending a lot of money for clicks from visitors who are not ready to buy. You might be spending a considerable sum with very little to show for that investment.

Certainly it would be ideal to show up in every search for every keyword, from the generic, informational stage, through the shopping phase, and right through to the purchasing stage and you may not be able to afford that . . . at least not at the beginning of your campaigns.

You may, in the beginning, need to focus on specific, longer keyword phrases—your *purchasing* terms.

Based on what you learn in SpyFu, your task is to do a cost/benefit analysis, choose the keywords you're going to focus on, and set a daily budget for each.

Then take the next step.

Google AdWords Traffic Estimator

Traffic Estimator (https://adwords.google.com/select/TrafficEsti matorSandbox) is the bid tool inside your Google AdWords account. This tool shows you the ***average clicks per day*** for your keyword terms at the amount you're willing to bid.

This is what SpyFu *doesn't* tell you. SpyFu gives you the bid range; Traffic Estimator tells you what traffic and clicks you'll get for a specific bid on a specific keyword or keyword group.

You will find this tool inside your campaign under the Campaign Summary tab. Here's your path: Campaign Management > Tools > Traffic Estimator; then you click on your Ad group.

You cut and paste your keywords and your bid into this tool, and it will estimate how many clicks you'd get at that bid price for that group.

From this information, you can quickly determine which words make sense for you and which don't, depending on your bid. You can also make bid adjustments until you get acceptable results.

Pick a term. Let's say *natural gas grills.* Pick a budget: let's say $1.00 per click feels comfortable for you. Traffic estimator will tell you that for $1.00, you will get X number of clicks and your position will be in the top three positions. If that seems like a good position and good traffic for you, and it's a price you're comfortable with it, then you're good to go with that term, that bid, and that budget.

And if you don't like what you're seeing, then you either pick a different keyword (if you're WAY off) or you begin to manipulate the variables on your chosen term until you get something that does work.

Adjusting Variables

One of the web content editors I periodically send work to was considering a PPC campaign. She did her keyword discovery, bucketing, and themeing. She came up with a budget that felt comfortable to her ($155/month or $5.00/day) and thought that $1.00 per click sounded about right as an amount she was willing to pay to get in front of a prospect. I was concerned that both her budget and her max click prices would be too low; however, we ran them in Traffic Estimator just as she requested them. The following scenarios show our results.

Scenario 1: Low Budget—Low Bid—National Delivery

We ran her top choice term *web site content editor* at her maximum bid (also called max bid or max CPC) at $1.00, with a daily budget of $5.00. With a campaign set at the national level, she'd be getting 2 to 3 clicks per day. That's too low a click volume to expect any conversions. **Likely outcome:** This campaign will probably not receive enough clicks for any conversions to take place.

Scenario 2: Higher Budget—Higher Bid—National Delivery

So we ran the same term *web site content editor* at $2.00 for her max CPC and a daily budget of $20.00 set at national level. Traffic Estimator showed us that this would double her clicks to 3 to 6 per day, and that's still too low. To make the most of a daily budget, you're shooting for the most clicks possible.

Scenario 3: Higher Budget—Higher Bid—State Only Delivery

Because this term *web site content editor* was important to her as the most descriptive term, we looked at what would happen if she started with her own state, rather than the whole country. She can always branch out later. Now her campaign suddenly

(continued)

> *(Continued)*
>
> started to make sense. At the state level (in her case, Oregon), she's getting good search volume. This didn't require narrowing her market to Portland, and we could have done that as well.

Delivery location is not the only variable you can manipulate. Your whole bucketed keyword list gives you all your other alternatives—narrower and narrower terms with longer phrases.

Here's another example of how you manipulate terms and variables to get to campaigns you can afford and that will deliver enough clicks to generate conversions. Let's say you sell supplements, and you find you can't really afford the keyword *supplements.* So you try *health supplements* or *energy supplements* or *men's energy supplements* and keep going until your bid and budget start to show a campaign that would make sense. Then, as you get data, you can refine this further. As you get sales and begin to generate income, you can broaden your terms to get in front of more people.

What you are after is the highest traffic term you can afford to get you the most visibility.

Traffic Estimator offers you that guidance. You set your bids, your budget and Traffic Estimator will tell you what you will get for that. You'll evaluate the numbers and make decisions on keywords, budgets, and bids based on the feedback that Traffic Estimator gives you.

The Challenge of Bidding

Bidding and budgeting in the PPC realm is not an exact science. There are lots of variables, and you don't really know what you're going to get or what it will be worth until you run your campaigns.

You have to start somewhere, and you have to make some intelligent choices. You want to go out of the gate with a compelling bid that will keep you online for a majority of the day and won't be used up in two clicks by 8:00 AM.

Assess your bids and assess your budget. How much can you afford to spend per day and what is going to keep you online for the longest time period or for a full day if possible?

Once you start researching terms in SpyFu and Traffic Estimator, you'll begin to get a sense of how the game is played and where you need to be for a campaign to make sense.

Setting a Bid

I do not recommend driving yourself crazy with specific bids on each keyword. If you spend all your time trying to pick the perfect amount, you'll never launch.

SpyFu gives you the range, *Traffic Estimator* tells you what traffic you'll generate, and yet you still need to select a number and start somewhere.

Let's say your keyword shows a range of $0.55—$0.97 per click. Set your max bid at $1.00 and see what happens. Don't try to get crazy with $.72 cents for second position. Pay attention to your personal bid and don't focus on what your competitors may or may not be bidding. Stay in your price range and budget.

Across-the-Board Bidding

At the beginning of a campaign, one approach is to simply start with a number that you feel comfortable with. That may be as low as $0.10 per keyword or $1.00, or significantly higher. You pick a number across the board for all your keywords, you throw it out there and you see what happens.

Sophisticated PPC marketers both use and recommend this approach. They advocate simply picking a flat rate for all keywords across the board, casting that net and seeing what you catch.

And it doesn't have to be a low rate to take that approach. Earlier, I mentioned a client who is in the business of solving complex tax problems for his clients. With his PPC campaign, he is willing to pay $20.00 per click to get his web site in front of a prospect. That's what targeted exposure is worth to him. He doesn't care that much where the other players are or who's bidding what. He sets his campaigns at $20 and runs them.

That is certainly one option, though even if you choose this approach, you may still want to run some of your terms through SpyFu and Traffic Estimator just to get a sense of the landscape.

Data

No matter which bidding tactic you start with out of the gate, after you run your campaigns for 24 to 48 hours, you will have a sense of the numbers, including:

- The number of impressions (times your ad appears in response to a search)

- Your average position on the page in the paid search results section
- The number of clicks
- And whether any of those clicks resulted in the visitor taking action on your site (conversions)

You have to get some data from your keywords and ads before you can make truly informed decisions about bidding. There's no crystal ball. You need to run your ads and keywords to see where you are on a page, which words are working for you, which clicks convert. Until you have that information, you're just shooting in the dark, so be conservative and circumspect.

In time, you will understand your company's threshold for how much you are willing to pay for exposure versus conversions. As you see the data come into your accounts, you will understand how to evaluate this.

Ongoing Bid Strategy

Once you have some data, you can begin to ask yourself a series of questions:

- What is a customer worth to me, that is, how much am I willing to spend to acquire a customer?
- What position on the page did my comfort-level budget get me? Is that acceptable? Did I show up *below the fold* (not visible without scrolling past the first screen)?
- Where are my competitors in relation to my ad?
- What can I comfortably afford on an ongoing basis?

The answers to these questions can involve making some hard decisions. Sometimes we just have to make peace with the fact that we can't always play in the same park and compete in the same league as bigger companies.

After a period of experimentation and data gathering, I counsel my clients that if they can't afford to be in the top three results for a given keyword, then it's time to ask: ***Is this the right keyword for my company at this time?***

Top three is generally where you need to be for the best results. If you can't afford that space, it may not be the keyword for you.

During this strategizing, it's important to identify what *kind* of keyword you're evaluating. Is it informational? Shopping? Buying? And the most important question of all:

Is this keyword targeted and converting enough that I'm willing to spend x dollars on this campaign/position? Is it worth this amount of advertising spend?

After you've answered these questions, then go back and set your bids accordingly. This process might require deleting some keywords from your account, temporarily pausing some campaigns, or tightening up some of your campaign settings (like timing, geography, or phrase matching) to maximize your return on investment.

At the end of the day, you must evaluate every keyword individually and decide whether you can afford that keyword. As you get further down the learning path, you can always add back in any keywords you decided to eliminate in the earlier stages.

Budgeting

If you're an experienced paid search advertiser, then you probably have a good sense of where to begin your budget settings. For a new advertiser, this task can be challenging.

First and foremost, only you know how much you can afford to spend on advertising for your business or organization. This line item on your budget is up to you.

However, within the general parameters you've set for advertising your business and the percentage of your advertising budget you've designated for Internet advertising, you probably have some legitimate questions for this particular medium.

How Much Should You Spend? How Much Is Enough?

The true answer to this question is that you won't know until you've run your campaigns for at least a couple of days. You have to start somewhere.

What I advise new advertisers to do is simply pick a number they can comfortably live with—an amount that will be okay with them when it shows up on their credit card—and run their campaigns with that budget for 24 to 48 hours. By then, you will have had some traffic and data and can make a more informed decision.

If $10 per day is comfortable, choose $10. If $50 works, choose $50. If $100 per day feels fine, go with $100. Keep in mind that you are setting this bid *per campaign*. So if you're running quite a few keywords, this will affect what you can afford for each one. If you're running a campaign in all three major search engines, that will also affect your budget. Calculate carefully.

Like bidding, budgeting is something you will get a feel for after you've been working with it for a little while and have some data on results.

Over time, you'll see through data analysis and performance what you can afford to spend on advertising. Make sure you set your budgets thoughtfully—and carefully—when you get to Chapter 13—Account Deployment.

Take-Aways

- The cost of a keyword is determined by bid, and also by many other factors including and not limited to how competitive and popular the keyword is, how many advertisers are bidding on the term, and page placement.
- Utilize SpyFu and Google AdWords Traffic Estimator to help determine your initial bids.
- Your goal is to bid on the highest traffic terms you can afford to get the most visibility possible.
- Be aware that budget settings in Google are DAILY maximums, not monthly.
- After launching your campaign, assess your bids and budgets to determine whether your keywords are targeted enough and are generating enough conversions to justify the amount you're spending.

Tools You Use in This Chapter
- SpyFu, Spyfu.com
- Google AdWords Keyword Tool, https://adwords.google.com/select/KeywordToolExternal
- Google AdWords Traffic Estimator, https://adwords.google.com/select/TrafficEstimatorSandbox

CHAPTER 13

Account Deployment

Taking Control

In this chapter, we finally get your pay per click (PPC) ads up and running. We are going to do more than just walk you through account deployment.

We are going to focus on how you, the advertiser, can and should take control of all the details of your PPC account and decide for yourself how to spend your money effectively.

Beware of Defaults

From a technology standpoint, the search engines make it as easy as possible for a novice advertiser to create a PPC account and set up ad campaigns. They provide great tools and tutorials to walk you

173

through the process, and they give you comprehensive instructions. They do such a good job, that I don't need to walk you through the setup; I can just confidently refer you to their step-by-step directions.

And that's great for both of us.

Except, they can't customize the settings for every advertiser. The automated setups they've created are designed with defaults that are intended to work across the board for all advertisers. Most advertisers just blindly accept the defaults on the account settings, and that can be a problem.

The search engines have no way of knowing your particular business and what does and doesn't meet your particular needs.

You don't need me to replicate the account setup, which you can easily follow on your own in Google; however, it is important that I alert you to the default account settings and the impact they can have on your campaign and its success.

My goal here is to educate you about the default account settings and the implications and effects of each of them, so that you can take control of your account and map out your specific road to PPC success. The best way to do that is to walk you through the account setup process.

Starting with Google

To intelligently discuss these default settings, the best approach is to walk you through the account deployment and account settings process. We're going to use Google AdWords (http://adwords.google .com/select/Login) as our example and starting point because:

- Google has the biggest market share as of our publication date.
- Google has the best tools for setup and account management.
- The AdWords account data can be exported from Google and migrated into the other engines.

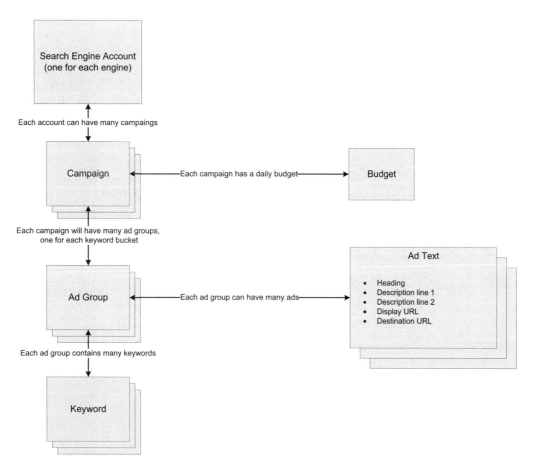

Figure 13.1   **Understanding Account Structure**

Google screenshots © Google Inc. Used with permission.

Anatomy of an Account

A PPC **account** can have multiple **campaigns,** which can have multiple **ad groups,** which can have multiple **ads,** which can have multiple **keywords.** Figure 13.1 is a visual representation of the structure for a search engine advertising account.

Road Map

Since we're starting with Google, here are the steps for setting up a live PPC account in Google:

1. Create a Google AdWords PPC Account.
2. Install Google AdWords Editor.
3. Build Out Your Campaign(s) in AdWords Editor.
4. Set Match Type in AdWords Editor.
5. Set Bidding in AdWords Editor.
6. Upload Campaign to Google AdWords.
7. Go through All the Campaign Settings.
8. Insert Conversion Codes.
9. Make Final Check and Activate.

Step 1: Create a Google AdWords PPC Account

If you don't already have an account with Google AdWords, now is the time to create it. Go to adwords.google.com and set up your account. There is a $5.00 setup fee. A credit card is required for billing and to activate the account.

Your AdWords account is usually funded in one of two ways: prepay or postpay. Both are charged to your credit card.

1. **The prepay option** lets you set a specific amount of money that you can spend each month. Once you've spent that amount, you are required to manually go into your account and add more money if you choose. Prepay works well because you have tight control on your spending; the downside is that you

run the risk of using up your money and halting your ads without knowing it. Also, it requires you to manually manage your funding. This option is similar to how prepaid cellular phones work. You add a certain amount of money into your account, and once you have used up the money, you can no longer make any calls until you add more money into the account. On the one hand, this is a great way to make sure that you don't have a nasty surprise at the end of the month; on the other hand, you might run out of minutes and you could miss an important phone call.

2. **With the postpay option,** you pay only for the clicks you've actually received, so you're not billed in advance. Google bills you after 30 days or when your account spending has reached your billing threshold, whichever comes first. This option is more automated. You give Google permission to bill your card for the activity your account generates within the parameters you have set up in your account. This option is a little like a traditional cell phone plan, where you pay for the minutes after you use them. As part of your account setup, you will be establishing a daily budget so you have control over the maximum amount that you will be spending.

For other billing options, please visit AdWord's online support at https://adwords.google.com/support.

WARNING

Your account defaults to ACTIVE once you set up the account. Make sure you put your account on PAUSE until you're ready to deploy it.

Step 2: Install Google AdWords Editor

The tool through which you will build your ad campaigns is called **Google AdWords Editor.** This is a free tool provided by Google. Once you build out your campaign, you can easily export it to Yahoo! and MSN. This is the great thing about Google AdWords Editor, and the reason you're creating your campaigns in Google first. Once you've done it in Google, you'll just export the information to the other two engines.

Another advantage of AdWords Editor is that it knows all the rules and editorial guidelines for your keywords and ad text. It will alert you to any errors in your ad text, including ad length, word usage, and invalid symbols. You will see a red (!) exclamation point if you violate any rules; and it will prevent you from uploading your account until the errors are resolved.

To set up Google Editor, go to *http://www.google.com/intl /en/adwordseditor* and download the Google AdWords Editor tool. There is an excellent "Getting Started" guide under its "help" menu. There are also great tutorials at http://www.google.com/support /adwordseditor. These will get you up and running in no time (see Figure 13.2).

Take the time to learn the basic functions of AdWords Editor. It's the foundation for all your campaigns. The balance of this chapter assumes you have become familiar with this tool, although we're still going to walk you through it.

Step 3: Build Out Your Campaign(s) in AdWords Editor

In this section, we discuss the basic steps for using AdWords Editor to build out your account. The first thing you're going to do is make sure you have two things by your side:

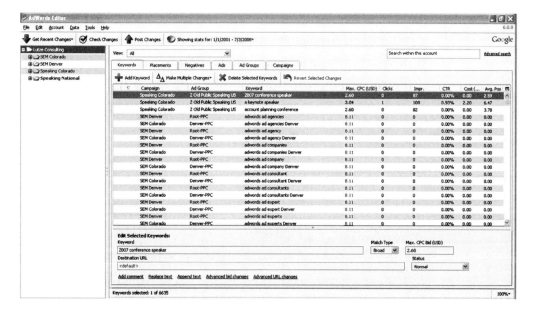

Figure 13.2   **Google AdWords Editor**

Google screenshots © Google Inc. Used with permission.

1. Your bucketed list of keywords that you have already chosen from your highest search volume terms.
2. Your ad matrix or whatever way you wrote the ads for each of your top keywords, including the destination page for each ad.

If you've already assembled these items as spreadsheets, great. If up to this point you have been more comfortable working on a legal pad, now is the time to get more high tech:

1. Open Google AdWords Editor.
2. The Open Account window will appear automatically when you open AdWords Editor for the first time. In the future, you can add accounts from the File Menu > Open Account.
3. Click Add Account.

4. Enter your AdWords advertiser login and password (from when you created your account) and click okay

5. If you currently have any campaigns under your account, AdWords Editor will automatically download these campaigns; however, we're going to assume you're starting from scratch.

Begin the Buildout Process

The next steps are as follows:

6. Open the Excel document or any document that contains your keywords and ad text.

7. Create a new campaign in AdWords Editor.

8. For each keyword bucket, create a new Ad Group inside that campaign.

9. Copy and paste from the keyword document, all your keywords by bucket into the respective Ad Group.

10. Copy and paste from the keyword document all negative keywords.

11. Create new ads for each Ad Group.

12. Repeat the process for all additional keyword buckets.

13. Make sure your campaign is paused before posting.

I'm not going to walk you through the details of these steps because Editor does that just fine without me, and I'm also assuming that you have familiarized yourself with Editor and have been through the "Getting Started" guide.

Step 4: Set Match Type in AdWords Editor

The search engines want to give searchers the best possible results for their searches. When an advertiser is asking the engine to display ads based on certain keywords, the engines like to make decisions about how to associate that keyword or keyword phrase with what the searcher just entered into the search box.

As an advertiser, you have to decide how much control you are going to give the engines in matching your ads to searches that are *related to or similar* to the keywords in your accounts. You do that by how you set your "match type" settings.

This is the first of the campaign settings that we alerted you to.

These settings need your attention because the default setting can hurt you.

Match Type Example

One of the keywords in my own account is "search marketing presentations." I can let the search engines decide what is and isn't a close enough match and when they should display my ad. Would I be comfortable with the search engines deciding *for me* that marketing presentations is close enough to search marketing presentations to call that a match? *Probably not.* Because even though it *appears* to the search engines matching software to be close enough—in reality it's not. Someone looking for a marketing presentation may not be looking for a presentation on search marketing at all.

If someone types in search marketing presenter, however, is that close enough to search marketing presentations? *Well yes.*

How about search engine marketing presentations? *Again, yes.*

So it's a tough decision and it takes some thought. The question is: Do you want the search engines using their best judgment about what's a good match and what isn't? It comes down to how much you trust the intelligence of the search engines.

And it's not a blanket yes or no decision. Numerous match settings are available with different degrees of control.

The *default* setting in Google is **broad match.** It's similar to **advanced match** in Yahoo! and MSN. This is the setting that allows the engines to match as they see fit using their own formulas.

On the other end of the spectrum is **exact match,** wherein you tell the search engines, in essence, "Only display my ad if the keywords match EXACTLY."

Match Type is one of those default account settings that might get you into trouble if you're not paying attention. You need to make a conscious choice about what works for you and your business. Also what works with your budget. A broader match setting means more matches and probably more risk of poor matches. What can your budget afford?

Match Setting Choices

Following are the match settings available to you in Google. The choices are similar in Yahoo! and MSN. Review them and carefully consider which is likely to be the best for you. You can always make adjustments after you see how your choice is working out.

Google Match Type Overview

Listed are the definitions for Google match types and how to use them with the keywords in your account:

- **Broad match:** This is the default option for all keywords. With this setting, if *widget* is one of your keywords, then your ad will show up any time anyone enters any term with the word *widget* in it. Your ad would probably come up for *blue widgets, red widgets, widget* without the s, and keywords that are like widget. You need to be careful with this match setting. If you don't sell *blue widgets,* you will be paying for clicks when you don't have that product to sell.

- **Phrase match:** If you select this option, and in your account you have the keyword phrase *blue widget* then you will only come up for searches that exactly match *blue widget.* The order and spelling are how phrase matches work. If someone types in *widgets, blue,* you won't appear. Or for *small widgets* or *red widgets* or *plain widgets* or any other *widget* phrase. The search engines will also look for broad matched combinations of *widget* only if they include *blue.*

- **Exact match:** This is the tight form of matching. So if you use [*blue widget*] then you will only come up for *blue widget,* and no other permutations of *widget* or *blue.* Most important, nothing can be put in between your keywords. There can be words in front and behind, however, not in between.

- **Negative keywords:** This match type is helpful because it excludes trademarks or styles/colors of products that you don't sell. If you sell *blue widgets,* and not *red widgets* and you put the word *red* in your negative keyword account, the search engine would know NOT to match you for a *red widget* search... even through the word *widget* is a match. (*source:* http://adwords.google.com/support/bin/answer.py?hl=en &answer=6100)

The Big Three use different terminology for these accounts settings. Google and MSN have you choose between *broad match, phrase match,* and *exact match.* Yahoo! has you choose either *advanced* setting or *standard* setting.

There are advantages and disadvantages to each setting. It's up to you to understand the differences among the settings and make the choices that are best for your business.

Further Discussion about the Broad Match Setting

If your account is set to broad match and you're using a term like *television* it's important to understand that *any phrase* with *television* in it can trigger your ad, including the word television with any word or words in front of it, behind it, or even in between it. The phrase *Sony television* would trigger your ad. So would *toy television* or *television parts* or *television repair.* Broad match is set for the most amount of traffic on the term. This can be dangerous—not to mention costly—because it can create the exact opposite of a targeted campaign.

You can protect yourself in a couple of ways:

1. Have a comprehensive negative keyword list so that any brand-names, makes, models or sizes you don't carry (or services you don't offer) are excluded and any other words or phrase that could modify your keyword into something you don't offer (e.g., parts, fake, toy, knockoffs, antennas, repairs) are also excluded.
2. Instead of choosing broad match, choose *phrase match* or *exact match* for your account. That stops the search engines from making matching decisions on your behalf. It also means that if there's a close match, your ad won't display.

In general, the search engines have good intelligence behind their matching software. And narrower match setting can really limit your keyword matches if searchers aren't typing in the term exactly as you've entered it.

Search Query Report

A Search Query Report is a critical resource, especially if you choose to run your terms on broad match. You can find this in the *Reports* section of your account. Your Search Query Report will tell you exactly how the search engines are matching your keyword or keyword phrase and you can see all the related searches. By reviewing this list, you can determine what matches the search engine is making on your behalf and if any of those matches are non-related. Any non-related terms you discover can be added to your negative keyword list. This makes a broad match setting much safer and minimizes your risk of bad matches and wasted clicks. I strongly advise running a Search Query Report at least every 30 days, and more frequently at the beginning of a campaign, so that you continue to add to your negative keyword list. It's the only way to make Broad Match really work for you.

Filtering

Match setting can be a tough call. You don't want to set it too broad or too narrow. I advise my clients to visualize their account as a gigantic strainer and their match settings as controlling the size of the holes. Imagine pouring in a whole bunch of keyword searches at the top.

Your negative keywords and your match settings strain out bad results. What you rule out makes the holes smaller so that what falls through is more defined and targeted and therefore more converting.

If you have an extensive negative list that you're confident about, you can run broad match with less risk of matches and associations you don't want. Otherwise, my usual recommendation to clients who are new to paid search advertising is to set their account on phrase match until they have enough experience to either narrow it down or broaden it up.

Remember:

- *Broad and advanced are the default settings* in all three search engines. If you want to narrow the field of where you're going to show up, *you have to go in and reset the match type manually.*
- If you're going to use broad match, your negative keyword list needs to be strong enough to filter out every possible match that you *don't* want.

Step 5: Set Bidding in AdWords Editor

We covered bidding in Chapter 12—Bidding and Budgeting—because we didn't want to spring something as complicated as bidding on you at the last minute, just as you were ready to deploy your accounts. Here, at Step 5 in deployment, you will go into each keyword and set your bids for each one. AdWords takes you through this process in a way that's easy to follow.

Step 6: Upload Campaign to Google AdWords

Now, in preparation for going live, we're going to upload your first campaign to the search engine. All the work you've done is currently sitting on your computer in your AdWords Editor program, and the search engine doesn't have it yet.

You're going to upload it by going to your Google AdWords Editor, logging in, and clicking on **post changes.** Don't worry, your account won't be active until you toggle your campaign to active; however, we're getting close.

Once you hit **post changes**, confirm that all your changes have been successfully uploaded and move on.

Step 7: Go through All the Campaign Settings

The account settings we review in this section often determine whether your account will perform for you or not. It's right here—in the campaign settings steps—that people often make their mistakes and oversights, and end up blowing their budgets before even getting in front of their best prospects.

The theme of this section is:

Those who pay attention to these details . . . win!

To get to your campaign settings, login into AdWords, click on your campaign name and click on campaign settings (see Figure 13.3).

Now, please pay careful attention as we go through each campaign setting in detail, because these details determine whether your campaigns will perform for you.

Budgeting Options

We talked about setting a budget in Chapter 12—Bidding and Budgeting. Here is where it comes into play.

All three search engines require you to set a budget. Note that the budget is a *daily* amount you're approving, not monthly.

As you can imagine, this is a campaign setting that can really hurt you, so enter your budget settings carefully for every campaign in your account, and then check them one more time.

If you're a new advertiser and picked your budgets fairly randomly without any real data, you will want to run your campaigns for a few days and then make use of the Recommended Budget tool that can offer you guidance on budget amounts.

Recommended Budget

After 24 to 48 hours, you can make use of a handy little tool in Google AdWords that will give you a recommended budget. However, you need to run the campaign for a few days before this can give you a suggestion based on your campaign performance.

To find this feature, log into your AdWords account, click on CAMPAIGN SETTINGS, then choose BUDGET OPTIONS, and then VIEW RECOMMENDED BUDGET.

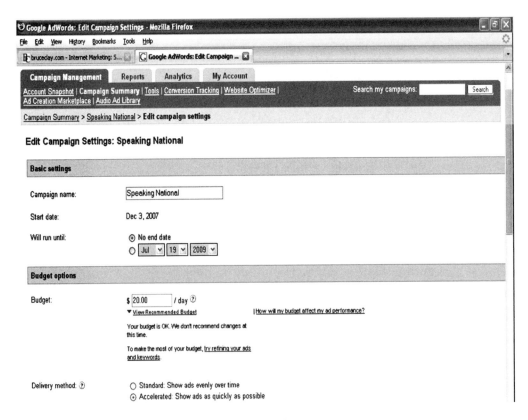

Figure 13.3   **Google AdWords Campaign Settings**

Google screenshots © Google Inc. Used with permission.

Figure 13.3   (Continued)

This will tell you the percentage of coverage you're getting at your current budget and will also give you a recommended budget for 100 percent delivery on your keywords. This number indicates what it would cost to have your ad display 100 percent of the time your keywords are typed into the search bar. One hundred percent delivery means your ad is displaying at every opportunity and you are receiving all the available impressions possible.

For a full explanation of how Google AdWords makes these recommendations, go to http://adwords.google.com/support/bin/answer.py?answer=8703&query=suggested+budget.

WARNING

Sometimes the **recommended budget** is a number that will make your heart stop. Don't panic! There are going to be some words you simply cannot afford 100 percent coverage on. If they're suggesting $500/day and you just don't have $15,000 budgeted for a single campaign over a 30-day period, then you're not going to do it. You have to decide what you can afford. However, the 100 percent coverage number is still excellent information. You'll know what percentage of coverage your current budget is giving you and where you'd need to be to get 100 percent delivery.

If the 100 percent coverage number is higher than you can afford, it's even more incentive for you to carefully consider every detail of every campaign setting so that you have narrowed down your audience as tightly as possible and are reaching carefully targeted prospects at optimal times and in optimal ways.

Paying close attention to any of the details in your campaign settings will help you leverage your budget to the maximum benefit, and will act as a filter that only lets the most targeted prospects through.

Delivery Method—Standard or Accelerated

How *often* do you want Google to display your ads? The obvious answer is all the time, right? Well, depending on your budget, you may not have enough money to give you 100 percent delivery in the search results 24 hours per day. If that's an issue for you, you need to carefully evaluate the **Standard** or **Accelerated** delivery method.

Standard Delivery Method lets you parse out your ad display throughout a 24-hour time period. This may display your ad every third or fourth time a keyword phrase is searched, rather than every time. This approach spreads the delivery of your ad in search results over the entire day.

Accelerated Delivery Method enables you to tell Google that you want your ad displayed *every time* someone searches under your keyword phrases until your budget is depleted. You do not want to miss an opportunity to be displayed even if your budget gets used up early in the day.

Recommendation: Use Standard Delivery Method if you are not running your ads only during certain hours of the day or not utilizing ad scheduling. Use Accelerated Delivery Method if you are using ad scheduling and you want your ad to display every time someone searches between the certain hours of the day.

Content Targeting versus Sponsored Network

Here you have to decide yes or no and then set content targeting to **on** or **off.** To help you make that decision, you need to know what content targeting is.

Content targeting refers to an option where you give permission for the search engines to display your ads on content-related, third-party sites. Instead of just putting your ad on an actual search result page of Google.com, they could decide to put it on a *partner* site that has content related to your ad. They might put an ad for camping gear on say a wilderness site. Or an ad for high-end cookware on a cooking site. The third-party site then chooses where the ad will be placed.

Here's the analogy I use to describe this approach: With a *sponsored search result* (where your ad shows up on a results page in direct response to a keyword search) you are like a bread supplier responding to a couple who come into a grocery store with a shopping list and bread is an item on that list. They know exactly what they want and need, and your bread product is going to be prominently displayed to them as they walk down the bread aisle.

Content targeting is more like the chewing gum that shoppers will throw in their cart while they're standing in the checkout line. They didn't go into the store to get gum. It wasn't on their list. However, there it is, and they go for it anyway as an impulse buy.

Only you know your product and market well enough to know which type of marketing is better for you and whether impulse marketing is likely to convert well for you.

WARNING

Sponsored search (ads displaying on search results pages) and *content targeting* (ads displaying on sites with related content) are lumped together inside your account, and content targeting is already turned on; *it is the default position.* Most people don't know about this, and so it just automatically runs. Like many default account settings, *you must make a specific adjustment if you want it turned off.*

Paid Placement Report

Google has a paid placement report that will give you a list of web sites that are displaying your ads if you've chosen content targeting. This list might also be an excellent way to police the sites costing you the most money, and then you can decide whether to exclude those sites from your content targeting.

In general, I recommend that new advertisers turn content targeting *off* on all three engines initially. I think you should have a fair amount of experience and data with sponsored search before you start testing content targeting.

Set Up Separate Accounts: Sponsored versus Content

If and when you decide to try content targeting, make sure to set up a *separate* campaign for it and manage that delivery separately from sponsored search. In your content targeting campaign, turn sponsored search off and just let your ads display on the content network. Treat your ad text and bids with the content targeting network in mind, and remember that this is an impulse buy. You will typically bid lower for keywords in content-targeted campaigns than for sponsored search because the searchers intent is more diluted. They're not on that site looking for you.

Ad Scheduling

This is an option in Google and MSN only. As of our publication date (Spring 2009), Yahoo! does not offer a scheduling option.

If you do nothing on this campaign setting, the default position is that your ad will run 24/7. This might be fine for you, *depending on the nature of your business.*

I know that when people are looking for a cleaning service, they almost always want to *talk* to someone about price or have a consultation. House cleaning isn't something they order over the Internet without a conversation. In that business, the inquiry aging is very fast. If a person is not there to answer the phone, the prospect will quickly find another cleaning service to call.

So I might suggest that they show their ads from Monday through Friday, from 9:00 AM to 5:00 PM, which is when someone is in the office to answer the phone and talk to prospective clients. A customer service representative that is good on the phone probably can close the deal and get a new client. So for a house cleaning company, paying for clicks outside normal business hours may not be the best use of a paid search budget.

Know what your prime time search hours are. They're very different for different businesses. For a service-based business, you might want to run your ads when someone's around to answer questions. If you sell fancy auto accessories and you know those kinds of searches are done after business hours and on nights and weekends, then you might want to take that into consideration. If your product or service requires a lot of research or comparative shopping that is probably also done mostly after hours or during breaks at work, so keep that in mind when choosing your ad scheduling.

When we take on a client account, we look at the hours that most of their online orders come in. It is very different for each client. Only you know your customers and their shopping patterns. And if you don't know, then start with 24/7 and see what the data tell you. *However, be aware of this account setting.* And if you're budget is tight, you might want to set your controls to a narrower window than 24/7. Remember, your goal is to *convert* as many prospects as possible and to maximize the return on your investment.

Rotate or Optimize Ad Text (Offered Only in Google)

If you are running more than one ad in any given ad group, this campaign setting lets you decide whether you want to rotate the ads evenly (the *rotate* option) or you want Google to pick the best performing ad and run that one (in which case you'd choose the *optimize* option). This option only comes into play if you have more then one ad in your campaign, which you may not have at the beginning. It allows all your ads to be tested to find the best performing text (the ad that gets the most clicks and conversions).

Google's default position is to optimize: they're choosing.

If I'm running two ads with two offers (free shipping/buy one get one free) I prefer them to rotate 50/50, and *I* want to be the one who analyzes the results. I want to see which one gets more clicks and more conversions and when—and I want to pick my own winner. Then I'd like to be the person to decide when I'm ready to optimize that one. Just remember, *the default is the optimize option,* so if you want to test different versions or offers, you need to set this option to rotate.

Geotargeting and Location Targeting

This option is covered in a fair amount of detail in Chapter 8— Location, Location, Location, now is when you have to make some firm decisions about *which geographic locations* you want to be seeing your ad or if you want to limit the ad geographically at all.

If you run a local ballet school in Orem, Utah, or you're a chiropractor there, you might want to geotarget your city so that only people in and around Orem will see your ad. If you have a trade school in Boise, Idaho, you might want to target all of Idaho. If you sell all-natural vitamins and supplements, the whole country might be your target audience. And if you sell incense from India, your potential visitors might be all over the world.

Once you decide *where* the people are whom you want seeing your ad, **be sure you set your geotargeting and location target-ing appropriately, or you will be paying for wasted clicks.** What are the chances that a nine-year-old in Hartford, Connecticut, will be attending your ballet school in Utah? Or that someone will drive from San Diego for even a great neck adjustment in Orem? If the answer is slim or none, then narrow your ads to your geographic audience. It doesn't cost you any money to do this, and targeting your ads in these cases will exponentially increase your results.

If you're not clear about the difference between *geotargeting* and *geographic modifiers* please go back and refer to Chapter 8—Location, Location, Location before deciding on how to handle this campaign setting.

Recommendation: If your situation isn't clear-cut, or you're not sure if geotargeting makes sense for you, I recommend a *U.S.*

Delivery campaign, which means everyone in the country will see your ad. You can always adjust this later.

Step 8: Insert Conversion Codes

At the end of the day, and especially after all the work you've done to create your ad campaigns, *you need to measure visitor response and results.* You'll want and need to know how often your ad is appearing, under what terms, whether searchers are clicking on your ad when it appears, and whether they're taking the desired action when they get to the page you've sent them to.

Whether it's to order a product, register for a newsletter, sign a petition, send in an application, call for more information, or fill out an inquiry form, you know what you want the searcher to do. Whatever your call to action is, you want to know if the person who clicked on your ad, did it. You need to be able to *track user behavior.*

The search engines have provided a way for advertisers to easily track conversions or actions from a PPC click. It simply requires that a **conversion code** or **conversion tracking code** be programmed onto your site. This code allows you to connect the dots from keyword phrase to ad text to final action on your site. It is invaluable for gathering critical data and helping you make intelligent decisions on which keywords, ads, and pages are getting you the results you want.

Many advertisers fail to add this tracking code to their accounts. Please don't be one of them.

Here's how to do it:

1. Inside your account, go to the **Campaign Management** tab, then choose the **Conversion Tracking** link on the top menu bar, and follow the instructions to **Create An Action** (see Figure 13.4)

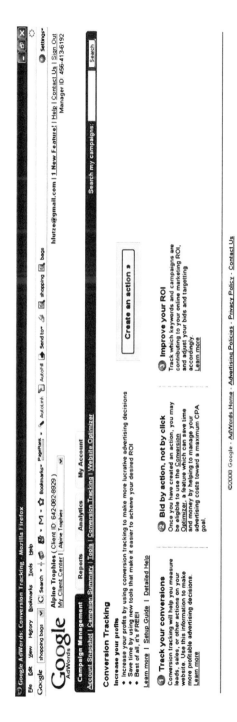

Figure 13.4 How to Set Up Conversion Tracking

Google screenshots © Google Inc. Used with permission.

Upon creating an action, the system will generate an account-specific conversion code. Here is an example of this code:

```
<!-- Google Code for Your Conversion Page -->
<script language="JavaScript" type="text/javascript">
<!--
var google_conversion_id = 000000000;
var google_conversion_language = "en_US";
var google_conversion_format = "1";
var google_conversion_color = "ffffff";
if (1500) {
var google_conversion_value = 1500;
}
var google_conversion_label = "lead";
//-->
</script>
<script language="JavaScript" src="http://www.google
adservices.com/pagead/conversion.js">
</script>
<noscript>
<img height="1" width="1" border="0"
src="http://www.googleadservices.com/pagead/conversion/
1068818650/?value=1500&label=lead&script=0"/>
</noscript>
```

You are not going to attempt to do anything with this code. You ARE going to tell your web designer that he or she needs to make sure *this code is placed on the confirmation page* of your call to action page.

The confirmation page is what shows up after the visitor has filled out the contact form, or the final shopping cart page of a completed order, or whatever you have asked them to do. This is the page that confirms that the action has been completed. On a shopping cart site, it would be after the credit card has been processed and you've provided an order confirmation. That page is where the conversion code resides and where it needs to fire. The code *does not* go on every page of your web site. ***It goes only on the desired end result page.***

This code enables you to track the most vital information that you, as an advertiser, could want. It is the only way for you to know which keywords are generating *business,* not just traffic. Your conversion code will tell you which clicks are *converting to customers.* You can't really evaluate a campaign without this information, so please DO NOT SKIP OR FORGET THIS STEP.

Step 9: Make a Final Check and Activate

You are now ready to launch your campaign(s).

Do a final check of every destination URL and make sure that it works.

Now you are ready to ACTIVATE all your campaigns that are currently PAUSED in your account. Your campaign will automatically be set to ACTIVE, unless you pause it. Then you can launch the account when you are ready.

Congratulations: You're off and running!

Take-Aways

- Use Google AdWords Editor to create, edit, and launch campaigns.
- Pay close attention to all your account settings and be especially aware of the "defaults." Failing to do so can cost you.

Tools You Use in This Chapter

- Google AdWords Editor, www.google.com/intl/en /adwordseditor
- Google AdWords Help, https://adwords.google.com /support

CHAPTER 14

The Care and Feeding of Your Search Engine Marketing Campaign

There are numerous advertiser mistakes I see over and over, and one of the most consistent is that advertisers think they can set up their campaigns and then they're done. They think the accounts can just run themselves.

They can't.

The care and feeding of a paid search campaign is a lot like the care of your car. It requires regular attention and ongoing maintenance to run properly. You have to keep putting gas into it; you need to change the oil and filters, rotate the tires, tune the engine, get it washed occasionally, and maybe even have it detailed.

201

You can't completely ignore your vehicle's maintenance requirements and expect it to keep performing for you—or wonder why it isn't working the way it should.

Campaigns must be watched, monitored, and managed. Just like with your car, ongoing care and maintenance is required for top performance.

There is a happy medium between setting your campaigns on autopilot and walking away, or watching them like a hawk every minute and driving yourself and everyone around you crazy, not to mention interfering with campaign performance.

Finding a Balance

In general, my advice to my clients is to start by checking the account twice a day for the first couple of weeks: once in the morning, once at the end of the day. That's plenty.

I know you've invested a lot of time, money, energy, and attention into this project, and constantly checking what's happening will not serve you. *Search engine rankings require time for your accounts to mature and build quality scores.*

If you look at them every 10 minutes to judge performance and start making changes, you'll never get a true performance reading. **You must let them build data including clicks, impressions, and conversions.** You can't be endlessly fussing with them.

This is not to say that if a certain keyword is running through your budget like gangbusters with no conversions that you shouldn't put that campaign on hold. Certainly use your judgment if something is way out of line. In general, you want to keep your ad text, bids, and keywords the same for a few weeks. Don't make alterations and adjustments too soon. You need to gather data before you begin to make changes.

Some things need time to mature, to blend, to meld, to reach their potential. Fine wine is one example. Luckily, campaign performance doesn't take that long. Cooking soup or a stew is probably a better example. You put in all the ingredients, and then you have to let it cook for awhile. You can't taste it every 10 minutes; you need to give it some time. And if you start tasting it and messing with it and adjusting the seasonings too soon, before the herbs and spices and meats and vegetables have had a chance to work together for long enough, you can ruin it. It may NOT need more onion or garlic or thyme or sherry or carrots—you must wait to see what happens when it has cooked long enough.

Let It Stew

It's the same way with your ad campaigns. Watch them, and don't make changes too soon. Wait to see how your hard work performs.

You're not in danger. Letting your campaigns run while you collect data isn't going to hurt you. We've guided you through the steps that will protect you. You've set your budgets to comfortable levels. You, not the search engines, are controlling all the details that could get you into trouble. So let's just take some time to see how the campaigns are going to perform. Let's see what the traffic and user behavior will tell us.

In the meantime, there is one thing you *can* do.

The Exception to the Rule

The exception to the *hands off for two weeks* rule is in the budgeting arena. If you had no idea where to set your budgets at the beginning of your campaigns, and you put in a comfortable daily budget number to start, then I advise you to check the *Recommended Budget* feature in Google after your campaigns have been running for approximately 24 to 48 hours.

You'll find *Recommended Budget* under Campaign Settings. We reviewed recommended budgets back in Chapter 12—Bidding and Budgeting. Now is when it actually comes into play because now there will be some real data on your account. When you go into the Recommended Budget tool now, Google can tell you what percentage of searches you are actually receiving at the budget you set.

The data might tell you that your Daily budget is okay. Or, it will give you a *Recommended Daily Budget* to provide 100 percent coverage (meaning that your ad would show up in 100 percent of the results for that search under those terms with that set budget). Beware, the budget number required to get 100 percent coverage may be way beyond what you can comfortably afford to spend.

What's important is that you know your own limitations, and that you understand your budget, the recommended budget, the gap between them, where full coverage lies, and what you're willing to tolerate in terms of missed opportunities.

And remember that, as you build customers and sales, you can close that gap.

Two Weeks Later: 80/20

Now that two weeks have elapsed since you went live with your paid search campaigns, it is the time to run an **All Time Keyword Report** from each of the search engines that you're running campaigns on.

Import those reports into an Excel document, and then sort by **clicks** and **conversions.**

See example report on FindAbilityFormula.com/Keyword Report.

Once you look at the data, you will begin to understand how the 80/20 rule tends to work in this case. You will discover that 20 percent of your keywords will give you most of the impressions and clicks and 80 percent will not perform as well.

The cream rises to the top.

And the cream is what we're interested in. Put your energy and analysis into that 20 percent. This is where searcher s are taking action.

Rebucketing

Next you're going to rebucket your keywords for optimum campaign performance.

First, you're going to take all the low-performing keywords—those on which you're getting zero search volume, zero clicks, zero impressions—and you're going to move them to a *Low Converting* or *Low Search Volume* campaign.

We don't recommend getting rid of them altogether because they may still present opportunities. You might have some long tail search terms that haven't received any impressions or clicks yet, and if someone *were* to enter that search string, you would probably net an excellent result. So you don't give up on them. You'll check them about once every month, and you'll just consider them low priority. Don't delete these terms. You can either re-bucket them in their own AdGroup or *pause* them to retain their performance history—if any.

Focus on the Cream

Next you're going to take your high-performing keywords—those that are getting good activity—and you're going to move them into a High Search Volume campaign so you can focus your energy on the keyword terms that ARE performing.

I suggest that you study the top 20 percent carefully and ask yourself these questions:

- Which keywords are my top performers?
- Am I paying too much for keywords that aren't generating *conversions*—not impressions and clicks, and actual *conversions*, that is, searchers taking ACTION on my site or landing page?
- Do I see any new ideas for *negative* keywords?

Once you've analyzed the answers to these questions, then it's appropriate, indeed wise, to start to make some changes to your account. I don't advise radical changes; however, some adjustments are often in order at this point.

Checkpoints

Here are some other things to pay attention to as you are analyzing your campaign performance:

- **Page position:** Where are you showing up in the results? The top three positions are usually best. If you're on a tight budget, you can settle for the top five, however, make sure you are visible above the fold before a searcher has to do any scrolling on the results page. Look at your position for each keyword in your account. If you're consistently falling below fifth position, you need to increase your max bid (the maximum amount you are willing to pay per click) for those keywords, you'll do this only for the top 20 percent of traffic generators.

- **Search query report:** A search query report will give you a comprehensive keyword list of all the associations being made to your broad match keyword phrases. This will help you better understand how Google is associating your terms with similar terms and also any possible negatives.

- **Ad text:** If you are running more than one ad per ad group and set your account to rotate for your ad text, exposure has been evenly split among your ads. Now is the time to look and see which ones got the most impressions, clicks, and conversions. If there are some clear winners, you need to change some of your campaign settings from rotate to optimize. You want the best ad to continue to be shown by the search engine.

- **Editorial status:** Make sure all your ads are working and none have been declined. Search engines have a list of editorial guidelines and can reject your ad if their guidelines are violated. Check periodically to make sure none of your ads have been declined for any reason. Guidelines are available for Google at: http://adwords.google.com/support/bin/answer .py?hl=en&answer=6313; for Yahoo! at http://help.Yahoo! .com/l/us/Yahoo!/ysm/sps/start/editorial/urls. html; and for MSN at https://help.live.com/Help.aspx?market=en-U.S. &project=adcenter_ContentAds_beta_ss&querytype=topic &query=MOONSHOT_CONC_EditorialGuidelines.htm.

- **Negative keywords:** Two weeks of data often provide you with new negative keywords to further refine the searchers you're getting in front of. Use Google's Negative Keyword Tool to keep building out better and longer negative keywords for optimal performance of your campaigns. Make sure you upload any new negative keywords to your Yahoo! and MSN accounts if you're running campaigns in all three search engines.
  — To find this tool, go to the Google keyword tool, then go to the drop down box for match type and choose negative. This will give you a suggested list of possible "negative associations" being made to your keyword phrases.
- **Keyword tool/keyword suggestion tool:** Maybe now is a good time to see if there are other keywords you might like to add, based on the keyword performance data you've gathered. A keyword suggestion tool can help you do this by suggesting terms related to your top-performing terms.
- **Landing pages:** If you created special landing pages for any of your campaigns, a few weeks into the campaign is a good time to evaluate landing page offers and copy:
  — Is your landing page working better than driving them to your home page?
  — If landing page conversions are low, look at the keywords you wrote for the page and make sure you are delivering what the searcher would expect on the path to purchase. Your home page might be a good destination for an information search, whereas a specific product search may be a great place for a landing page test.
- **Checking your quality score:** See if the user experience you have set up is tight and refined. If you have done your homework, you will be rewarded with great or okay quality scores.

Checking Your Quality Score

Check your quality score on each keyword in your account and see if your scores are *great*, *okay*, or *poor*.

Our information from Google is that it takes about two weeks to establish a quality score you can trust. Once you have your accounts running for a couple of weeks, you can check your quality score by going to your Google AdWords account where your keywords are displayed, choosing Customize Columns, and selecting Show Quality Score from the drop-down box.

Understanding your quality score is important. It's good to know your ratings and why you have the ratings you do; then you can try to improve any elements you can control—particularly the relevance of the page where the searcher will land.

Obviously, you're shooting for scores that are all *great*, and you want to refine your users' experience until you get there. However, a great score is not always possible, so strive for the best you can achieve. A great quality score can mean a higher position on the page at a lower cost. Of course, a great user experience is also important for conversions!

The best advice I can give you about quality score is to repeat what I said in Chapter 11—After the Click—By focusing on your users' experience and delivering the best and most relevant results to them, you are doing the most important thing you can to achieve the highest quality score.

Tweaks and Refinements—30 to 60 Days

Now that you've been up and running for about a month, or maybe for a couple of months, you've learned a lot about how pay per click

(PPC) campaigns work and which keywords are performing best for you.

If you want to keep growing your campaigns and achieving ever better performance, you will need to keep refining your keywords and adding new ones, expanding your negative keyword lists, and honing in on other variables. Here are some tips for doing so:

- **Negative keywords:** At the beginning of every month, check for new negative keywords from the previous month's data. Every 30 days, you have a new group of people searching and more data for searches that weren't good matches. Google will show you the matching they did for all your core terms, and you'll be able to see which ones weren't really a match for you. If your account is set on *broad match,* you have to keep checking this information and adding new negative keywords. So that you don't forget to check this, set a Calendar Reminder in your e-mail program.
- **New keywords:** I advocate checking for new keywords every month. The Keyword Discovery tool will show you how. Google now gives you search data numbers as well in its Keyword Tool. These are great resources for capitalizing on seasonal trends, keywords you may not have thought of, and new keywords in your industry. It's a useful way to keep building out your top 20 percent performers. Keep abreast of the new keyword tools because they keep getting better and better. Check my podcasts (ppcpodcast.com) for updates on the newest and best tools.

What about the Other Search Engines?

Although at the time of this publication, Google has the largest search market share and is the easiest to get started with, you may want to consider running campaigns in other search engines.

For the most up-to-date search engine market share to date, visit the following sources or search for the keyword phrase *search engine market share*:

http://www.searchenginewatch.com
http://www.marketshare.com

When you're ready to branch out, take what has worked for you in Google AdWords and move the data over to other search engines such as Yahoo! and MSN.

In the following section, I offer some suggestions for enhancing your search engine relationships with Yahoo! Search Marketing, and MSN adCenter. Certainly adding new search engines means more work for you or your campaign manager; however, it does represent additional opportunities for reaching your target audience.

Ongoing Support

The Big Three search engines all offer various tools and options for account and performance support.

- **Google Ad-Ons:** These include Keyword Expansion Reports, and Ad Text Writing tools. You can specifically request that these features be added to your account.

- **Google Optimization Request:** Even the smallest of advertisers can request an optimization of their accounts from Google AdWords customer service. Google prefers that you have a specific business objective for requesting the optimization. They will in turn give you suggestions for ad text, keywords, and additional settings to improve your campaigns. This is only allowed on a case-by-case basis for each account.
- **Content and Site Targeting:** You may want to consider trying to test content targeting in a separate and unique campaign from your sponsored search campaigns. Bid them lower than sponsored search and watch carefully. Research "Site Targeting" and add this as well. You can handpick sites that have similar content that might be a great complement to your site. Make sure you are bidding for the top three positions as most content partners only display three ads on their sites.

Search Engine Relationships

Building relationships with the people at the search engines is important. Initially, your only access to the company will be through the engine's basic call center, and as your ad spend increases, you'll get better levels of customer service.

What you aspire to is a one-on-one relationship with a search engine representative or group of representatives working for your account.

Agencies with greater *ad spend* per month get greater levels of support. You may not have as much clout as an independent advertiser; however, that does not mean you can't request help.

Begin to build a relationship with someone and ask for that person's direct line. Take care of the people who help you as they take care of you. Send thank-you notes, tell the manager how great the reps are, send a Starbucks™ card to a rep who does something special for you. Get the benefit of the rep's knowledge and in turn, treat them well.

Here are some of the differences among the perks the Big Three offer:

- **Yahoo! Search Marketing:** If you spend more than $500 over a three-month period consistently, you become a "Gold" advertiser and you get a bit of special treatment. Gold members are given a special 800-number served by a small group of experienced professionals. They also get expedited requests on their accounts and quicker editorial review for new campaigns. Ask your account rep if you meet the criteria to be upgraded to Gold account status.
- **Google AdWords:** This search engine also offers upgraded attention to its bigger spenders. Even if you don't hit that mark, you can still build relationships and request help with spreadsheet uploads, keyword expansion, and so on. Google will limit how much they'll give you for free based on your spend level, and you can usually find people who will help you. Befriend them.
- **MSN adCenter:** As of the publication date of this book, MSN adCenter offers something called Quick Start, which provides someone to help you through your initial campaign launch. MSN also has released a fabulous keyword tool called MSN adCenter Excel Add-In that gives you real-time data from MSN Live and.Net accounts.

More Help and Support

While we're on the topic of help and support, if the care and feeding of your campaigns should become more than you can comfortably handle yourself or with existing staff, you may want to consider getting some help—either in the form of additional in-house staff person, a search marketing agency or consultant.

If you decide to get some assistance either now or in the future, Chapter 15—Hiring Help—offers some guidance for hiring.

Take-Aways

- Campaigns don't run themselves; you have to monitor and manage them for optimal performance.
- Management includes ongoing evaluation of results by clicks and conversions.
- Focus on your top performing keywords, ads, ad groups, and campaigns.
- Use a keyword suggestion tool to expand on terms related to your top-performing keywords.
- Add to your negative keywords to further narrow your prospects.
- Managing a campaign is an iterative process of tests, tweaks and refinements.

Tools You Use in This Chapter
- Google Editorial Guidelines, http://adwords.google.com /support/bin/answer.py?hl=en&answer=6313 or http:// tinyurl.com/googleeditorial

- Yahoo! Editorial Guidelines, http://help.Yahoo!.com/l /us/Yahoo!/ysm/sps/start/editorial/urls.html or http:// tinyurl.com/yahooeditorial
- MSN Editorial Guidelines, https://help.live.com/Help. aspx?market=en-U.S.&project=adcenter_ContentAds_beta_ ss&querytype=topic&query=MOONSHOT_CONC_ Edito rialGuidelines.htm or http://tinyurl.com/msneditorial

CHAPTER 15

Hiring Help

Paid search campaigns require monitoring, maintenance, analysis, care, and feeding. You can't just set the ads to run with no one monitoring them. That's a surefire road to disappointing results.

Setting up these ad campaigns and walking away is a poor Internet marketing strategy. They need attention and fine tuning. Only you can know how much time you have or are willing to put into your search engine marketing. Only you can know whether it makes sense for you take time away from your core business to manage your pay per click (PPC) campaigns or whether you need some help, either internally or outsourced.

However, someone's got to be minding the store.

You'd be shocked to see some of the things that my agency discovers when we get hired to fix a company's accounts. We start with a complete inventory of all the campaigns and often find that there are no negative keywords in the account, no tracking codes, and no conversion tracking. Or they are running high-level informational keywords. Or even though the target audience for the business is local, no geotargeting has been set.

Someone set the vehicle on cruise control and no one was in the driver's seat. Yes, the car can *run* on its own; however, it can't steer itself, and without a driver, it's highly unlikely that the car will reach its desired destination. Crash and burn is the most likely outcome for this scenario.

So please make sure that someone is in the driver's seat. If not you, then you have the following choices:

- Hire an agency or independent consultant.
- Hire an experienced search marketing employee.
- Train someone in-house to manage your campaigns.

Decisions, Decisions: Outsource or In-House?

If your overall business plan includes PPC and search engine optimization (SEO) as key marketing strategies and you're committed to search engine marketing (SEM) for the long run, I suggest you invest in training and empowering someone within your organization. Whether you choose a new or existing employee, it requires an investment of time and money to train that person in search marketing.

The agency option is probably a little bit easier, though I must caution you not to be too hands-off.

Hire an Agency or Independent Consultant

An agency can be a great option if paid search is a short-term strategy, your internal resources are either strapped or limited, or this is a core competency you don't want to take on.

Hiring an agency might be the best option; however, you can't just turn over your account and walk away.

There are a lot of things you now know that an agency either doesn't know or may not do, and you will have to be on top of them about many of the details you've just learned.

Just as you monitor the performance of other account professionals in your life (e.g., your accountant, your stockbroker) and keep them apprised of your aims and goals, give them directions, and make decisions—even though you hired them to be your advisors—you should have a similar level of involvement with your search marketing agency.

Anyone advertising on the Internet needs to understand the basics of search marketing and can responsibly direct a campaign themselves, direct an employee, or direct an agency. If you don't take responsibility for understanding the search medium and how it works, how are you going to hold anyone you hire accountable? And without that, you're sure to get hurt. Protecting business owners from that outcome is one of the main reasons I wrote this book.

Don't Assume

To assume that a search marketing agency will be doing everything right and that they can be trusted completely is a big error.

Trust me, most agencies are taking the path of least resistance and effort; they're doing the easiest and most obvious things, and more often than not, *they're not paying attention to some critical details.*

I don't want to give agencies a bad name; it's just that some of the things I see in this arena are just plain shocking. And not only are small agencies making these mistakes. I see this in multimillion dollar businesses who have hired big-time, well-known advertising and SEM companies to manage their search engine advertising.

I once met with a big media company whose agency—I kid you not—had no conversion tracking on any of their campaigns. They also had no negative keywords in their accounts, and all their campaigns were running on broad match. This was a $25,000 *per month* SEM account that the agency was handling, and none of these details were being properly managed. Imagine the care and feeding of the agency's smaller accounts!

Restore Trust

This is part of why search marketing firms and the search marketing industry in general have such a spotty reputation. Indeed, another reason I wanted to write this book was to restore some credibility to the industry, which has been profoundly injured by the businesses that have gotten burned by search marketing and search marketing agencies.

I spend time with clients every day simply trying to restore their trust in this advertising medium. I want to evangelize a better approach to search engine marketing. Whether advertisers are running campaigns themselves or using an agency, I want to see consumers protecting themselves by getting educated about this medium. It is every advertiser's responsibility to learn about our profession, and it is our profession's responsibility to lift the veil and educate our clients.

Okay, I'm off my soapbox now. Thanks for listening.

What to Look for in a Paid Search Marketing Agency

If you want to hire an agency to manage and oversee your paid search campaigns, interview candidates very carefully. Make sure they are knowledgeable, experienced, and above all, trustworthy.

There are horror stories aplenty out there, so be diligent in your screening.

Here is the approach I recommend:

- **Find out how many years of experience the agency has and how many clients they've served.** Unlike other industries, there aren't a lot of veterans in paid search because it is still a relatively new field. If you can find someone who's been around for awhile and has a bit of knowledge under the belt, it can serve you well. However, just because people say they've run PPC campaigns before, doesn't mean they're experts. Ask them to be specific. How many clients have they served? Managing an AdWords campaign one summer for their dad's lumberyard isn't exactly depth and breadth of experience.
- **Check references.** Ask for three or four names and numbers. Make sure you to talk to a few of their *current* clients, and that they are showing measurable returns and are happy with their service levels.
- **Check accreditations and affiliations.** Is the agency part of SEMPO (Search Engine Marketing Professional Organization)? Make sure that the person managing your account has the following (very important) *credentials:*
  — Google AdWords Certification.
  — Yahoo! Paid Search Affiliate or Ambassador (which requires passing an exam).
  — MSN qualified.
- Then find out if the agency or your account manager has Google, Yahoo! and MSN agency-level support and will they be providing you with privileged VIP access to the search engines?
- Ask about their system for ongoing reporting and whether they report weekly or monthly.

- Do they do keyword build-outs and create new keywords lists based on historical clicks in your field.
- Are they completely plugged in to all the latest and greatest features of each site's paid search offerings and do they take on the responsibility of keeping you abreast of those service offerings? (This is important because these change rapidly and you want your agency to be your information source.)
- How do they charge? The most common formulas are:
  1. An up-front or optimization fee to get your accounts up and running or adjusted.
  2. A percentage of spend, commonly a 5 percent or higher percentage fee that is charged each month for each search engine where you have an advertising account.

Which you choose will depend on your style and situation. If you just need your account optimized on a one-time basis, and once it's handed back to you, your internal people can take it from there, then you'll want to choose the up-front/optimization approach.

If you don't have internal people who can oversee your campaigns, you'll want a hands-on approach for managing your accounts on a daily basis, and that's where a "percentage of spend" per month might be a good way to go.

This is an outsourcing situation you have to be careful about. Just because they call themselves an agency, doesn't mean they are. On the one hand, they may just be working out of a basement somewhere as a start-up. On the other hand, they can be young and working from a basement and still have had a good deal of experience that is getting great results for their clients.

The only way to know is to ask a lot of questions, check references, compare performance, and compare price quotes to be sure you're getting what you want and need.

The In-House Option

Finding someone who knows how to manage paid search campaigns is challenging. In the future, it will probably be easier; however, paid search is still a relatively new and rapidly changing field, and few experienced professionals exist.

Often, the job of managing the company's online paid search marketing campaigns and accounts falls to the youngest or newest employee with computer expertise. You figure they know computers and they grew up surfing the Internet. Maybe that makes them a good candidate to oversee your paid search; maybe not.

Yes, they've grown up on Google; however, they're also the most inexperienced in the workplace, and deliverables aren't always their strong suit. Often these workers are cocky and think they already know everything about computers. Paid search is a science unto itself. So if you're going with young computer whizzes make sure they are open-minded and trainable and don't think they already know everything about everything.

The other common knee-jerk reaction is to assign the project to the company's Information Technology (IT) person or whoever's in charge of the web site.

I am challenging you not to do either without some conscious thought.

Here is what I recommend: See if you can find someone in your company with outstanding computer aptitude who understands and knows your business well and someone who has constant interaction with sales or customer service.

You might also consider your marketing manager if that person is Internet savvy.

Search engine marketing, especially paid search, is an exciting, growing, up-and-coming industry. Many of your employees (especially younger employees) will be interested in this project.

Training

No matter who is in charge, training is important. If you're committed to advertising your company on the Internet, the employees in charge need to know what they're doing. Spending a certain amount of money each month on paid search without also investing in someone to take care of it is a mistake. Setting up your accounts and then walking away from them doesn't work. **Someone has to manage the operation.**

And they need to be taught how to do that. You can't just push them into the deep end of the pool and expect them to know how to swim.

You're going to have to send your designated manager to a workshop, a training session, maybe even a conference or two, so he or she can learn the current methods, strategies, tactics, and tricks of paid search. PPC Summit (PPCsummit.com) is great (and it just so happens I teach there); you can find other training offers, workshops, seminars, conferences, and summits at searchenginewatch.com.

Otherwise, you'll be in for some unpleasant surprises, underperforming campaigns, and a lot of wasted money.

Training Guidance

In his or her first year, send the online advertising manager (even if it's you) to a search marketing conference or summit.

Industry Conferences to Consider
- SES Search Engine Strategies, searchenginestratedgies.com
- SMX Search Marketing Expo, searchmarketingexpo.com
- PPC Summits, PPCSummit.com
- PubCon, PubCon.com
- OMS Online Marketing Summit, onlinemarketingsummit.com

These programs have different tracks: business to business (B2B), business to consumer (B2C), Beginner, Intermediate, or Expert. Review the offerings with your designated manager and pick and choose carefully with them which classes and tracks will best serve your company before they leave. Create a specific agenda and send your manager with specific goals: Find a tool for "x", learn how to do "y", or they'll be completely overwhelmed at the conference. It's also a better return on your investment. You're paying for the training, so you get to tell them what you want them to come back with. Don't just let them loose.

These industry trainings are high energy and exciting. Not only will your staff come back with a comprehensive understanding and a specific set of skills, they'll also come back charged up, excited, and ready to take on your search engine marketing.

Also, if you can hire an agency to coach that person for a few weeks through the early stages of a campaign, that kind of hand-holding can be invaluable.

As business owners, you must learn to prioritize your time. If PPC starts devouring more hours in the day than you should give it, you need to get some help.

Take-Aways

- If managing your PPC campaigns is more than existing staff can handle, you can hire a campaign manager in-house or outsource to an agency or consultant.
- If you hire an agency, carefully check their experience and credentials; however, you will still need to oversee their work.

(continued)

(Continued)

Don't assume they know everything we've taught you in this book.

- If you choose the in-house option, the campaign manager should be given extensive SEM training.

CHAPTER 16

SEO—Search Engine Optimization

After going through the hard work of creating, conducting, and managing your pay per click (PPC) campaigns and finding out which keywords consistently produce conversions (visitors who take ACTION), you are ready to undertake the challenge of search engine optimization (SEO): getting your pages ranked in the *organic* or *natural* listings so that you don't have to pay for clicks forever.

To reiterate what we have said throughout this book, although everyone would like to start with these free listings, you need to start with PPC to get your hard data, and then you convert that knowledge into an SEO campaign.

And even then, SEO cannot be counted on as a reliable or consistent performer; however, that's another book. Reliable or not, SEO is an integral part of SEM, which requires a two-pronged approach for true success: PPC and SEO.

Basically, what you are going to do now is take your top-performing keywords and re-create your web site to optimize its findability under those terms. That almost always requires new web site design, or at least new navigation and organization; carefully crafted customized content, specific linking strategies, and other tricks of the trade to get and keep your site highly ranked in Page One results.

It is beyond the scope of this book to walk you through the intricate steps of undertaking a successful SEO campaign.

What I *can* do is introduce the high-level concepts so that you understand the factors that influence search engine rankings. I can also outline the basic mechanics of SEO so that you can intelligently direct your in-house people, your web designer, and your SEO agency or consultant throughout the SEO process.

What Search Engines Care About

The search engines primary responsibility is to provide relevant search results for keyword searches. They are the keepers of the content and deliver that content to users in response to their searches.

The search engines must be vigilant about making sure that all 10 positions they deliver for search results are the most credible sites available. They build your trust (and their reputations) by doing this search after search. Their business model is predicated on this relationship of trust.

Every time you search on Google, Yahoo! and MSN, you are trusting them to give you relevant search results pages that are not filled with spam, non-relevant pages, or just junk.

And by and large, they have delivered. The reason that *Google* is now a verb as well as a noun and that you *Google it* when you want information about something is that you get back, generally, exactly what you asked for. Search engines are reliable resources for good information. If they weren't, people wouldn't use them. However, they do. According to a 2007 comScore study (http://www.clickz.com/showPage.html?page=3627303), roughly 750 million people worldwide over the age of 15 conducted a search on the Internet in the month of August alone.

The public expects that when they enter a search term (keyword or keyword phrase) into a search box on a search engine, they will get back relevant results that directly answer their need, all within seconds.

Maintaining this reputation is of primary concern to the search engines.

Your Primary Concern

As a business owner, what you care about is showing up on Page One of those search results so that you are easily FINDABLE for your prospects. You want Page One visibility for all the search terms that get you web traffic and conversions (purchases).

What Is SEO?

Search engine optimization (SEO) is the art and science of aligning what the search engine wants with what you want.

If your web site is the most relevant result for a searcher's keyword, then all parties get what they want: You get Page One visibility; the visitor gets the most relevant response to their search;

and the search engine delivers a perfect match, which is what they're after.

This alignment is achieved through the use of keywords.

Wikipedia defines Search Engine Optimization as "the process of improving the volume and quality of traffic to a web site from search engines via 'natural' ('organic' or 'algorithmic') search results for targeted keywords."

The alignment of your web site with your converting keywords in conjunction with what the searcher needs or wants in alignment with what the search engines want to deliver is what SEO is all about. That's how you end up with a good position in the *natural* or *organic* results.

You SEO (optimize) your pages through keywords, and you figure out which keywords work for you by getting hard data from your PPC campaigns.

PPC + SEO—The Marriage of Two Enemies

Those *free* listings go by many names. *Search Engine Optimization (SEO), Natural Search, Ethical SEO, Organic Search, Organic Results,* and so on. To make life easy, we're just going to call it SEO.

SEO and Paid Search are often viewed as being in opposition to each other, and nothing could be further from the truth.

Internet marketing success lies in the marriage and balance of these two elements of search engine marketing.

Remember, this book is called *The Findability Formula*. Your goal is for your customers to FIND you on the Internet, and that happens through both PPC *and* SEO.

Although your eventual aim is to pay for ads less and less as your organic rankings improve over time, your Internet marketing will almost always remain a delicate balancing act between PPC and SEO to ensure consistent top positions for your key search terms.

Your goal with all your Internet marketing is to show up on **Page One** for your highest performing keywords.

PPC guarantees that . . . for a price.

SEO is much less certain, and if you can get there and stay there, you don't have to pay when searchers click on your listing.

Although every keyword is going to have a different landscape, ideally, you would have a paid search ad at the top of the paid search results and an SEO entry at the top of the organic search results, thus doubling your presence on each results page you've targeted.

Over time, if your organic ranking stays pretty steady, you can start to diminish your paid ads. This is how paid search and SEO work together and why they should be tracked and managed together.

You will probably never achieve top organic rankings under every keyword term in your paid search account. You're probably always going to have some paid search campaigns running for your key search terms.

Your goal is to reduce the paid and increase the organic results over time. You start with paid search, and as your organic rankings climb, you pay less and less for your paid search.

The Big Picture

Let's get real: if you try to go after an informational keyword like *Search Engine Optimization* or *Mortgages* you will almost certainly fail. These keywords are the high traffic, low conversion terms. We've already talked about this in depth in reference to your PPC campaigns. The same principles apply here.

Much of what you've learned thus far—especially your keywords—will become the foundation of your SEO strategy. The detailed execution of an SEO campaign is beyond the scope of this book, and in this chapter, we provide an overview of the steps and offer tools and resources to guide you when you undertake your SEO work.

Tools You Can Use

A successful SEO effort requires the use of some third-party tools. The search engines do not provide the tools to optimize your site. They provide tools to track your progress, however they don't teach you how to get there.

There is no manual for SEO, however there are some great tools available. In my experience, the Bruce Clay (www.SEOToolSet.com) SEOToolset® and methodology is outstanding. It has been the best match for my consulting business because of the results it produces for my clients. A week-long training and certification program is available as well as online tools to guide you through the SEO process. I am biased in favor of the Bruce Clay™ approach, and in the interest of fairness, I also offer other suggestions, some of which are free or low cost. However, you'll need to research those on your own.

SEO Road Map

Here are the basic initial steps you must undertake to begin a SEO project:

Step 1: Theme web pages with converting PPC keywords.
Step 2: Run multipage keyword density analysis.

Step 3: Edit title and meta tags.

Step 4: Write new web site page copy.

Step 5: Update new title, meta tags, and page content.

Step 6: Submit your revised web site to search engines.

Step 7: Track your results.

Step 1: Theme Web Pages with Converting PPC Keywords

Page theme means taking related keyword phrases and matching them to a relevant content page on your web site. This page is then specifically targeted by keywords so it is found in a search engine result.

Themeing is important because search engines do not have *real* intelligence, they simply have software programs referred to as spiders (albeit sophisticated ones) that determine what a page is really about by judging its content. Spiders only pull the data of the page back to the data center where a sophisticated algorithm is run to analyze it. Just as you can confuse a person by talking about too many things at once, you can easily confuse a search engine spider by covering too many topics on one page. Your goal in themeing is to define every page of your web site by consistently using two or three keywords that directly relate to the content of the page, and represent the page theme. The spiders then get a clear and consistent message when they read (also called crawling or spidering) your page.

Here's a simple analogy. If you sell bananas, apples, and oranges, and every page is a fruit salad that includes all three fruits, you haven't delivered a clear message. Better to have a separate banana page, an apple page, and an orange page, so that when the spiders are checking for banana content, you come across as a good result; and when looking for apple, you have a clear, focused page about apples. If every page is a mishmash of fruits, the theme gets too diluted and makes high ranking elusive.

Figure 16.1 is an example of a web page with no themeing.

Figure 16.2 is an example of a page with SEO themeing.

In your PPC accounts, run an *All Time Keyword* report to see all your top performing terms. Then, map out your web site in a diagram similar to that shown in Figures 6.1 and 6.2. Pick two or three related keywords that are your best performers by (1) conversion and (2) clicks. Then page by page, match your top performers with content-related pages. If you do not have a page that is content related, it might be time to create a new page for your site.

Map every page in your site. You may want to exclude Contact Us, Privacy, and FAQs as these pages are not typically content-specific pages.

Now you have a plan by which to execute your SEO. Lay out your document using a site mapping tool; Microsoft PowerPoint also has a great organization chart tool.

Step 2: Run Multipage Keyword Density Analysis

http://www.bruceclay.com/newsletter/volume42/keyword-relevant-content.html

Keyword density is one of the factors that search engines use to evaluate the relevance of a page. According to *Wikipedia: **Keyword Density** is the measurement in percentage, of the number of times a keyword or phrase appears compared to the total number of words in a page. In the context of search engine optimization keyword density can be used as a factor in determining whether a web page is relevant to a specified keyword or keyword phrase.*

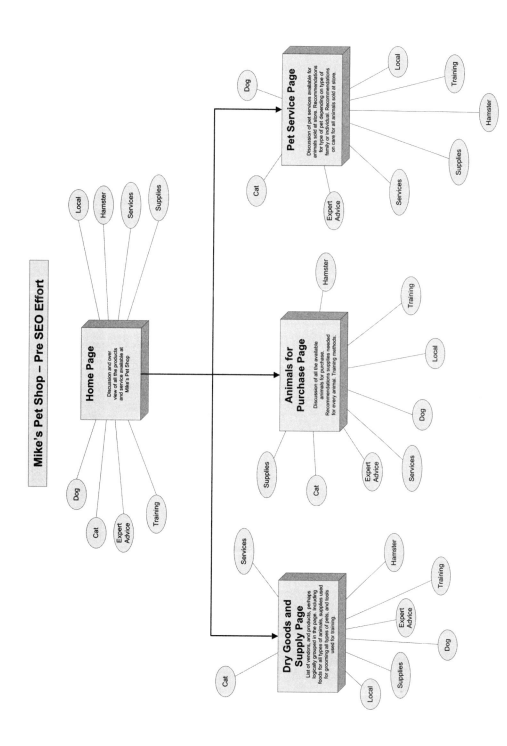

Figure 16.1 Overview of Site Theme Pre SEO

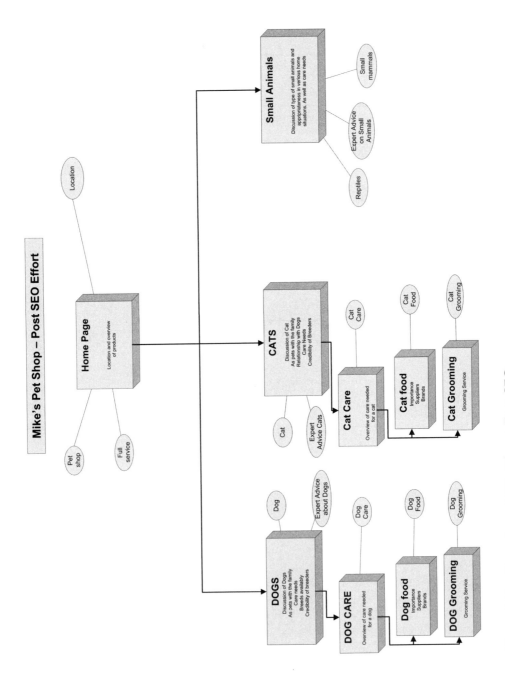

Figure 16.2 Overview of Site Theme Post SEO

Keyword density is not about loading your site with a keyword over and over. That is poor user experience, and the search engines work hard to exclude spammy content from their search results. Not only will you fail to achieve the placement you're after, you might not achieve any placement at all.

So how do you achieve keyword density that will get your good positioning? I use the Bruce Clay SEOToolset® Keyword Density Analyzer (KDA) and would recommend you research this as an option at www.seotoolset.com. Although the full version of this tool set isn't free, there is a free version at http://www.seotoolset.com/tools/free_tools.html. Additionally, if you search the Internet under the term keyword density analysis, you should find many free services that you can use to run this diagnostic evaluation for your site pages.

Run the diagnostic for every page or page theme in your site themeing document. The Bruce Clay SEOToolset® multipage KDA is my favorite because it takes the top seven web sites under a given keyword phrase, runs a keyword density analysis for that keyword, and builds a custom recommendation by which to meet or beat that percentage on your page, without risking so much repetition that you'd get rejected as spam.

The search engines are not going to tell you the exact configuration to get your page ranked under a particular keyword, and because all seven of the sites are already ranking under your term, this tool analyzes these pages and determines the commonality of the collective. Then you write your pages in alignment with what's already there. Go for a median approach first. You have to set yourself equal before you can prove yourself better. This puts your pages in contention with the other top-ranked sites. Table 16.1 shows an example of a diagnostic.

Table 16.1 **Example: Personal Injury Attorney**

Recommended "personal injury attorney" Configuration

	META Title	META Description	META Keywords	Head Tags	<!--Comment-->	ALT Codes	Hyperlinks	First Words	All Body Words	ALL Words
Page total word usage	11	18	46	12	1	15	1	200	615	719
attorney	9.1% (1)	5.6% (1)	4.3% (2)	33.3% (4)	100.0% (1)	13.3% (2)	100.0% (1)	1.0% (2)	0.8% (5)	2.4% (17)
injury	9.1% (1)	5.6% (1)	6.5% (3)	16.7% (2)	100.0% (1)	6.7% (1)	100.0% (1)	2.0% (4)	1.6% (10)	2.8% (20)
injury attorney	18.2% (1)	11.1% (1)	4.3% (1)	66.7% (4)	200.0% (1)	26.7% (2)	200.0% (1)	1.0% (1)	0.7% (2)	3.6% (13)
injury lawyer	18.2% (1)	11.1% (1)	4.3% (1)	16.7% (1)	200.0% (1)	13.3% (1)	200.0% (1)	1.0% (1)	0.7% (2)	2.5% (9)
lawyer	9.1% (1)	5.6% (1)	4.3% (2)	8.3% (1)	100.0% (1)	6.7% (1)	100.0% (1)	0.5% (1)	0.3% (2)	1.4% (10)

Here's a guide for making sense of the shaded row on the table:

- **Meta Title** should be 11 words long, utilizing the words *personal injury attorney* in this order and mixed up such as *injury attorney* and its variations.
- **Meta Description** should be 18 words long utilizing the words *personal injury attorney* and its variations.
- **Meta Keywords** should be 46 words long and keyword variations.
- **Head Tags** (H1, H2, H3, etc.) in your HTML should be 12 words in length.
- **<!– Comment –>** tag is one word long. Comment is just a notes area that the web designer can use for date of design, copyright, and so on.
- **Alt Code or Alt Text** is the text you see when you mouse over an image—15 words in total across all images on the page.
- **Hyperlinks** should have one instance in the anchor text or clickable text of the link.
- **First words** inside the <body> tags, the search engines like to see keyword rich data in the first 200 words.
- **All Body Words** should be, based on your competitors' body copy, 615 words with variations of *personal injury attorney* and its variations.
- **All Words** in the entirety of the page should be a total of 719 words. If you add up all the elements in the recommendation excluding first 200 words, you will end up with 719. Stay focused on columns 2 thru 11. Understand that they are the totals for words on your page.

The object of this section is not to overwhelm you with details; it is to show you how to optimize your pages to be competitive. For you to be considered for Page One visibility, you must mimic some of the attributes of the other top 10 results, and keyword density reports tell you what you need to do to achieve that. This is the only way the search engines will view your site as a contender for page one rankings for your chosen terms.

Step 3: Edit Title and Meta Tags

First of all what is the title and what are meta tags? The title and meta tags are HTML codes that give the search engines an idea of the nature or theme of the page. They are located in the head section of the page code. Historically, meta tags were significant factors for ranking and relevancy purposes along with the title tag, which still plays a predominant role.

Do meta tags still matter? Yes and no. They're not weighted as heavily as they used to be; however, they are still part of the criteria. They are only one of the elements search engines look at to determine the content and theme of your page. Not every search engine considers meta tags equally; however, why take chances? I recommend doing them anyway.

No one knows exactly all the criteria for page ranking, although Google states they have 200+ ranking signals (http://www.google .com/corporate/tech.html). If meta data is one of them, why not include it? No matter what your webmaster may say, you should include unique description and keyword meta tags. Make sure they are set up and written to match the page themes from your theme-ing document. Work with your webmaster on the actual code or research HTML code to insert into your pages.

Step 4: Write New Web Site Page Copy

Whether you hire a professional web site copy writer or you endeavor to write this content yourself, the keyword density recommendations should be the guiding force behind your strategy. You can provide the data to your content writer, have him or her read this chapter, and then work together to achieve the numbers, or you can write the content yourself. In either case, your goal is to come as close as possible to the target numbers, and you can make your own judgment call on the length of your pages.

If the recommended word count for your home page body copy comes in at 2,000 words, you need to ask yourself if that many words will provide a good user experience. If the answer is no, it would just be for the search engines rankings, you may want to satisfy the site visitor by having fewer words. You want to meet or slightly beat the recommended numbers, and there are exceptions. Take it one page at a time and use your judgment. Remember: *Customer First, Search Engine Second.*

Step 5: Update New Title, Meta Tags, and Page Content

If you do not update your own web site, give your updated page titles, meta tags, and copy to the person who maintains your web site. After you have been notified that the changes are complete, you might want to check to make sure they didn't take any liberties with your updates.

Step 6: Submit Your Revised Web Site to Search Engines

- http://www.google.com/addurl
- http://search.Yahoo!.com/info/submit.html
- http://search.msn.com.sg/docs/submit.aspx

> **WARNING**
>
> Submit your pages only ONCE to each search engine. We will give you a tool to check to see if your pages have been spidered and indexed.

Step 7: Track Your Results

These sites will help you track and verify your submission. They will also help you set up advanced tracking tools to check elements like robots.txt, site maps, and more. Review the tutorials for each of these tools; they are a wealth of information.

- Webmaster Tools, http://www.google.com/webmasters/tools
- Yahoo! Site Explorer, http://siteexplorer.search.Yahoo.com
- MSN Webmaster Center, http://webmaster.live.com

After you have submitted your pages and are tracking your status with the three major search engines, you need to find a reporting tool that will give you your rankings by keyword. If you subscribe to the Bruce Clay SEOToolset®, you will get the ranking and monitoring you need to track your progress. There are also hundreds of other tracking software packages that are online or downloadable. They will run daily or weekly to give you reports on your ranking by keyword and other valuable reporting data. Here's a resource for finding those tools:

- **Mike's Marketing Tools—Search Ranking Software Resources,** http://www.mikes-marketing-tools.com/ranking-reports

Remember, patience is key. Don't expect to see ranking improvement immediately. It takes time for the engines to index your site, trust your site, evaluate its worth, and determine if it deserves placement on page one as a super-relevant result for a particular keyword. I usually tell my clients that this process takes three to six months, depending on the competitive nature of the keyword. (Thankfully PPC is nearly instant!) You will notice when this time frame has ended, as your pages start to move toward page one visibility. BE PATIENT.

Linking

When we talk about linking, we mean an *inbound* links from other sites as well as internal links between your own pages. Because these are seen as forms of endorsement of your pages, the search engines factor links into your rating/ranking/score. The more links you have, the more important the search engines rate your site.

Not All Links Are Created Equal

Some of the best possible links are non-reciprocated links from high ranking web sites using the linked text with your keyword phrase also known as *anchor text*.

Example

A pet shop that wants to be found under the search term *pet shop Denver Colorado* would want links using the words *pet*

(continued)

> *(Continued)*
>
> *shop Denver Colorado* from web sites and especially those that rank high for that particular keyword phrase. A good example for this pet shop would be the USDA (U.S. Department of Agriculture) web site (USDA.gov). It sends a subtle message that USDA *endorses* this puppy mill-free site and links to it on their certified pet shops page with the keyword *pet shop Denver Colorado.* This is the brass ring of links. Because the site doesn't have a link to USDA on its site, this one-way link is called a non-reciprocated link. This is the highest level of endorsement one web site can give to another.

Although valued by the search engines, reciprocal links communicate less value than one-way links because reciprocal links cancel each other out. Trading links with another web site provides a good user experience for your visitor rather than just a link for search engine rank.

Link Hierarchy
1. Links within your own site pages
2. Inbound, non-reciprocated links
3. Reciprocated links

Your linking goal is to get as many links from other web sites keeping the link hierarchy in mind. Ultimately, any link is a good link as long as it comes from a reputable web site.

When it comes to linking, your ongoing, never-ending job is to keep your eyes open and your radar out for getting as many high-quality links as possible. Every partnership, vendor, new client, or marketing effort is an opportunity for you to request a link back to your site. Always ask; the worst they can say is *No.*

SEO Wrap-Up

I hope this chapter has enabled you to understand the basics of optimizing your web site and will empower you do it yourself or hold your SEO vendors accountable for their approach and the campaign's performance. Don't take for granted that they know how your business should be found in the search engines and what terms are your best keywords. By reading this book, you now know enough about search engine marketing to guide them.

The Findability Formula Wrap-Up

My intention for this book is to equip you, the reader, with fundamental concepts, strategies, and action steps so you will now have the ability to manage your PPC and SEO search marketing campaigns.

For too long, businesses of all sizes have been operating in the dark when it comes to SEO and PPC. I am a strong advocate for educating about all aspects of search engine marketing. I hope this book blazes new trails on that path and sets a new ethical standard that holds search engine marketing (SEM) vendors accountable for their services.

This book is also a guide for undertaking a PPC ad campaign and for translating what is learned from PPC into successful SEO efforts. In addition, the book illuminates the relationship between

PPC and SEO, and clarifies that successful search marketing is not about one or the other, it's about their ongoing dance with each other to dominate the search results pages.

I hope this book helps you take control of your search engine marketing and empower you to reject meaningless technical jargon, and instead actively seek understanding of the search medium and how it relates to your business.

Your ultimate goal is to differentiate yourself from your competitors and make sure your web site is found by leveraging the search engines. Remember, searchers can't become customers unless they find you.

Never stop learning and making the necessary changes to achieve top rankings for all your top converting keywords. I wish you the best, and I will see you at the top.

Invitation

I encourage you to register at www.FindabilityFormula.com for updates, articles, coupons, tools, podcasts, and other valuable information that will keep you, your team, and/or your agency on the leading edge of SEM strategies.

If you found value in what you have learned, please post a review of the book on Amazon.com or any other book review site you like. Don't forget to link to my site using *internet marketing book*.

I will be looking for your questions, success stories, and learning's. E-mail me any time at heather@FindabilityFormula.com. If you send me a testimonial and the keyword you would like me to use to link back to you, I will be happy to post it on my web site/blog.

Take-Aways

- Once you know your top-performing keywords, you can apply this knowledge to a SEO campaign
- SEO is not an exact science. The site that pays attention to the most details wins.
- We know that good rankings depend on many factors, but chief among them is providing *relevant* and rich content to create a good user experience.
- SEOToolset® is a comprehensive tool for tracking, monitoring, and analyzing your SEO efforts.
- Linking is another important component of SEO.
- For the best overall search marketing results, PPC and SEO should work together to produce optimal visibility on search results pages.

Tools You Use in This Chapter
- Bruce Clay SEOToolset®, http://www.seotoolset.com
- Bruce Clay free tools, http://www.seotoolset.com/tools/free_tools.html
- Google Webmaster Tools, http://www.google.com/webmasters/tools
- Yahoo! Site Explorer, http://siteexplorer.search.Yahoo.com
- MSN Webmaster Center, http://webmaster.live.com
- Robots.txt generator, http://www.mcanerin.com/EN/search-engine/robots-txt.asp
- Ranking Reports, http://www.mikes-marketing-tools.com/ranking-reports

Index